T0368080

THE MEDIATION MINUTE:

Insights on Alternative Dispute Resolution

Scott I. Zucker, Esq.

authorHOUSE®

AuthorHouse™
1663 Liberty Drive
Bloomington, IN 47403
www.authorhouse.com
Phone: 833-262-8899

Published by AuthorHouse 09/26/2024

ISBN: 979-8-8230-3378-7 (sc)
ISBN: 979-8-8230-3377-0 (e)

Library of Congress Control Number: 2024919269

Print information available on the last page.

Mediation: a means of resolving disputes outside of the judicial system by voluntary participation in negotiations structured by agreement of the parties and usually conducted under the guidance and supervision of a trained intermediary

Merriam-Webster

CONTENTS

FOREWORD

When I started practicing law in the late 1980's, the term "ADR" (alternative dispute resolution) was still foreign to most lawyers. It was certainly not a system discussed or taught in law school and not often raised as an option in the midst of initiating a lawsuit, and certainly not while the matter was pending. Settlement negotiations were handled directly between the advocating lawyers as compared to working through third party neutrals and the thought of using a paid arbitrator rather than a judge to create binding awards was considered outlandish (and in some jurisdictions illegal).

Over the last thirty plus years, the concept of ADR has flourished. A majority of businesses include arbitration provisions in their consumer, commercial and employment contracts and, typically, the right to enforce these provisions has prevailed in the courts. And certainly, more and more matters are resolved every day through the use of either court ordered, community based or private, voluntary mediation services. Mediation, by study and survey, has been credited with a success rate of settlement and resolution of disputes exceeding eighty percent. Mediation works, especially if it is done correctly.

THE MEDIATION MINUTE: Insights on Alternative Dispute Resolution is a compilation of articles written over the past few years as I have learned more and more about the process, strategy and psychology of successful mediations. The topics are varied and hopefully some of the discussion points will assist both lawyer-advocates and other mediators to consider issues that may assist them in achieving better outcomes in their next mediation.

At the end of the day, the concepts of self-determination, confidentiality and communication are the bedrock of any mediation or negotiation effort. If those tenets are followed, the opportunity to use a third party neutral to help disputing parties reach a resolution of their differences should result in a positive closure to the pending conflict.

Always remember, whether you are an advocate or a neutral, you are helping people (businesses are people too!) resolve their problems. That's a big responsibility and must be carefully managed with professionalism and ethical consideration. I hope these articles can be helpful and useful in reaching those goals.

Scott Zucker

Mediation: It's All in the Style

Mediation is a very effective way to resolve disputes between parties. Certainly, there are many reasons why mediations may work, even in strongly contested matters. In some instances, it is the first time that the parties have had a chance to tell someone their "story". And oftentimes, just sharing a parties' perspective about the dispute can be the first step in helping to reach its conclusion.

The method of mediating a matter, depending on the parties involved and sometimes the type of dispute, can also impact the ability of a matter to reach a resolution. That method, or the particular "style" that a mediator may use to facilitate a resolution session, can be the difference between a case that gets resolved and one that falls apart.

Here are the typical methods of mediation being used:

1) Facilitative. This is the most common style that is used, where a mediator will "facilitate" the negotiation process between the parties. The facilitative mediator will first have each side

tell their story and then will typically have the parties break into private sessions or caucuses to consider their respective positions. The facilitative mediator will then "shuttle" between the different parties with a goal of assisting each side to move in a direction to help create a solution that both sides will accept. The facilitator seeks to enhance the communication and understanding between the parties. Although the facilitative mediator may ask questions, the mediator does not offer the answers. The facilitative mediator also does not offer opinions or predictions regarding the resolution of their case but helps each side "communicate" to each other through the mediator concerning the facts in dispute. Facilitative mediation is process-driven, in that the facilitator manages the process, but it is up to the parties to work towards a self-created resolution.

2) Evaluative. The evaluative mediator is one that will express their opinion concerning the advantages and disadvantages of each side's case to help both sides understand the risks inherent in pursuing their case to closure in front of a judge, arbitrator or jury. The evaluative mediator can often help move one party that is stagnant in their position once that party hears from a "neutral" party the weaknesses of their case. The evaluative mediator can offer the parties an independent cost-benefit analysis to the case at hand, and can ultimately provide their opinion regarding the ultimate outcome of the case. For this reason, the evaluative

mediator can often be considered "heavy handed" in their management of the process since one party may feel that the mediator is not truly being impartial due to their assessment of the case. To be a successful evaluative mediator, that person needs to have a level of experience and knowledge that is sufficient to sway the parties to understand the risks of not resolving their case while it is still in their control to settle.

Although these methods are primarily the most common ones used by mediators, over the years there have been some efforts to expand the approach towards resolution and therefore a few other styles have evolved. Those additional methods have been called both "Transformative" or "Narrative". The transformative mediator approaches the dispute with the goal of helping to repair the broken relationship between the parties as a means of then helping to resolve their underlying dispute. The transformative mediator focuses on having the parties share their values and interests with the other side. Some transformative mediators have a background in mental health or psychology and are successful in connecting with the parties on an emotional level in order to help create a resolution to their dispute. A narrative mediator is someone that seeks to reshape the existing conflict by giving it a new "narrative". The goal is by reshaping the story, the parties can see the dispute in a new light and hopefully find a new approach from that new perspective to help settle the matter. Although these other methods may be considered "idealistic", it is often times the most successful mediator that will be flexible during the mediation process and utilize all the tools in that mediator's toolbox to help find an approach that leads to a successful resolution of the parties' dispute.

Ethics in Mediation: Principles That Impact Both the Mediator and the Participating Parties

There are clear guidelines that a mediator must follow as part of a successful mediation process. Of upmost importance is the *impartiality* of the mediator, demonstrating a lack of bias for any party or issue that may be raised during the mediation session. Inherent in that position of impartiality is the avoidance of any conflict of interest, even if slight, that might hinder the openness of either party and impede the potential success of the process. Second to the necessity of impartiality is the requirement for *confidentiality*. A mediator must clearly seek to demonstrate that information being discussed with one party is not being shared with the other party unless instructed to do so by the protected party. Again, without confidentiality as part of the process, the parties will likely be hesitant to share information that might be the essential to reaching a resolution. Lastly, a mediator should avoid any suggestion that he or she is providing legal advice or *counseling* the parties as part of the process, avoiding any impression that the mediator is challenging the legal positions taken by the parties' counsel if represented or inferring the validity of claims being asserted by a pro se party. Although it is appropriate for a mediator to offer comments regarding the relative positions taken by the parties during mediation, that evaluation should be limited to the recognition of the inherent risks of litigation. Even in confidential caucuses, a mediator should avoid any appearance of acting outside the role of a neutral intermediary, regardless of whether a request is made by a party seeking the mediator's opinion on the merits of a particular case.

All of these guidelines are part of the central foundation of the mediation process and each includes a level of ethics that must be maintained to uphold the integrity of the process. While these guidelines are focused on the role and actions of the mediator, the parties also share ethical duties when participating in mediation. The parties must recognize that, even though the mediation is not in front of a judge and no oaths are taken, it is crucial that the parties demonstrate **honesty** in their representations and seek **fairness** in the ultimate resolution of the dispute in order for the process to work. Mediations will not work if the parties involved actively make statements or present positions that are untrue or unsupportable. Similarly, mediations will not work if the parties involved seek harm against the other party or insist on taking positions based on malice rather than goodwill.

The principles of **respect, justice, shared well-being and integrity** are crucial values that are inherent in a successful mediation process. These ethical standards are not unique to the process of dispute resolution, but are hopefully built within the community norms and rules that individuals apply in their everyday practices. It is always disappointing when disputes arise and litigation ensues, but one of the reasons that mediations, as well as other forms of alternate dispute resolution, work is that the participants ultimately seek truth, fairness and goodwill in the result. If the parties come to the table with these ethical considerations in mind, the disputing parties should be able to factor these standards into their decision making and reach a principled and mutual resolution that provides benefits for all concerned.

Georgia Enacts the Uniform Mediation Act

Effective July 1, 2021, Georgia became the thirteenth state to enact the Uniform Mediation Act (the "Act").[1] The Act, which was drafted in cooperation between the American Bar Association's Section of Dispute Resolution and the National Conference of Commissioners on Uniform State Laws, offers uniform standards for mediators and parties who agree to participate in mediation or other alternative dispute resolution (ADR) programs. It was created to provide clarity on certain issues of mediation, such as the privilege of confidentiality, and has ultimately been adopted to promote the use of the process. If a party is concerned about a possible lack of confidentiality during a mediation/ADR process, the incentive for candor and honesty, both essential parts of any fruitful discussions, may be lost. The Act provides guidance on privileges against disclosure, admissibility and

---

[1] Other States that have enacted the Uniform Mediation Act are Nebraska and Illinois (2003), Iowa, New Jersey, Washington and Ohio (2005), Utah, Vermont and the District of Columbia (2006), South Dakota (2007), Idaho (2008) and Hawaii (2013)

discovery as well as the rules relating to the waiver and preclusion for confidentiality. The Act provides a clear privilege that assures confidentiality in legal proceedings, creates limitations regarding allowable disclosures by mediators to judges who may rule on the pending case and requires mediators to disclose potential conflicts of interest. The Act's goal is to enhance public confidence in ADR by supporting confidentiality, promoting open communication and strengthening the integrity of the mediation process. There are definitely benefits to having a main body of law governing all aspects of mediation within a state rather than having potentially conflicting rules between court and private mediation programs. Uniformity of the rules and procedures creates clarity with respect to conflicts in jurisdictional enforceability as well as international acceptance (the Act also provides for the adoption of the United Nations Commission on International Trade Law).

The Act spells out what confidentiality in fact means with regards to the parties, non-parties, lawyers, as well as the mediator. Ultimately, information shared during a mediation would be considered privileged and confidential, unless this right is waived by all parties to the mediation. Furthermore, any information shared during a mediation would be deemed inadmissible for use at trial and otherwise not subject to discovery. Finally, the discussions that occur during mediation would be viewed as protected, equivalent to the attorney-client privilege.

Relevant sections in the Act include the definition of a "mediation" as a "process in which a mediator facilitates communication and negotiation between parties to assist them in reaching a voluntary agreement regarding their dispute" and the definition of a "mediation communication" as a "statement, whether oral or in a record or verbal or nonverbal, that occurs during a mediation or is made for purposes of considering, conducting, participating in, initiating, continuing, terminating, or reconvening a mediation or retaining a mediator".

The following privileges apply under the Act:

1. *A mediation party may refuse to disclose and may prevent any other person from disclosing a mediation communication;*
2. *A mediator may refuse to disclose a mediation communication and may prevent any other person from disclosing a mediation communication of the mediator; and*
3. *A nonparty participant may refuse to disclose and may prevent any other person from disclosing a mediation communication of the nonparty participant.*

The Act also clarifies that there shall be no privilege for a mediation communication that is:

(1) In an agreement evidenced by a record signed by all parties to the agreement;
(2) Available to the public under Article 4 of Chapter 18 of Title 50, relating to open records, or made

during a session of a mediation which is open, or is required by law to be open, to the public;

(3) A threat or statement of a plan to inflict bodily injury or commit a criminal act of violence;

(4) Intentionally used to plan a criminal act, to commit or attempt to commit a criminal act, or to conceal an ongoing criminal act or criminal activity;

(5) Sought or offered to prove or disprove a claim or complaint of professional misconduct or malpractice filed against a mediator;

(6) Except as otherwise provided in subsection (c) of this Code section, sought or offered to prove or disprove a claim or complaint of professional misconduct or malpractice filed against a mediation party, nonparty participant, or representative of a party based on conduct occurring during a mediation; or

(7) Sought or offered to prove or disprove abuse, neglect, abandonment, or exploitation in a proceeding in which a child or adult protective services agency is a party, unless the public agency participates in the Division of Family and Children Services mediation.

Georgia already has a longstanding structure to govern and control the management of mediation and alternative dispute resolution in the State as provided by the Georgia Supreme Court. The Georgia Supreme Court Rules address the qualifications to be a neutral, including the ethical standards for neutrals and the educational and training requirements to be approved. The approval of the Act in Georgia is unlikely to contradict the intended goals and procedures of the Georgia Supreme Court Rules.

Anyone acting as a mediator or participating in a mediation after July 1, 2021 should review the Uniform Mediation Act and be comfortable with its requirements. The Act adds a new chapter to Title 9 and is labeled under O.C.G.A. §9-17-1 through §9-17-14.

The Importance of Preparing Mediation Statements

Before discussing the benefits of pre-session mediation statements, it is important to qualify what a mediation statement is and how it is intended to work.

First, a mediation statement should be an objective outline of the facts and law relating to the dispute at issue. Mediation statements should not be written the same way an advocate would write a motion for summary judgment or a brief on a compelling legal issue. Instead, a mediation statement should ultimately be written to create a possible road map of the facts and legal issues in contention, not only for the benefit of the mediator who will be helping the parties resolve their controversy, but also to help educate the other parties as well.

Second, to be effective, mediation statements should be openly shared between the parties in the dispute. Why? Because if the mediation statement does its job outlining the relevant facts and law it might go a long way toward influencing a party's willingness to negotiate during the mediation process.

With that plan in mind, mediation statements should be written knowing that it is going to be read by the other parties in the case. A mediation statement is not the place to be argumentative or disparaging to the other side about their case, but instead it should create a demonstration of the strength of the case being presented. Further, by exchanging the statements, parties may avoid the issue of new information being presented at the mediation which could delay the ultimate ability of the parties to reach a resolution during the actual mediation. Mediation is not the time to reveal last-minute surprises. It will more often hurt a case rather than help it. A mediation statement should be a positive way for each side to enlighten and inform the opposing party about the elements of their case to aid in their consideration of whether they should settle to avoid the risk of trial. Sometimes mediation is viewed as free discovery. Such an approach may help the litigants learn what each side knows to help weigh whether a case should be settled before or after discovery has been conducted. As part of that approach, in order to be truly helpful and effective in the mediation process, mediation statements should be shared.

For clarity, the shared use of the mediation statements should not waive the confidentiality of the mediation process itself and should be protected within the boundaries of that confidentiality (therefore should not be discoverable for use as evidence at trial). Even if the mediation statements are shared, there is still plenty of room during the mediation process to make certain things confidential.

Mediation statements can fortify the willingness of the parties to reach a resolution. The language that is used in the statements can clarify the intent of the party to work towards compromise, without worrying that their openness would be seen instead as a weakness. Through a well-drafted mediation statement, the demonstration of that receptiveness can add a positive tone to the settlement process.

If you step back from the mediation process and recognize how it typically functions, it is clear how helpful it might be for the parties to provide mediation statements in advance of the meeting. Without the benefit of prepared mediation statements from both sides, the parties might ultimately be left with a verbal confrontation between the competing parties and the hope that the mediator will be able to decipher enough of it to help guide the litigants to a resolution. A stronger approach is to lay the cards on the table and openly discuss the facts and the law that apply. Hopefully, by taking such an approach, it will allow all parties to properly judge the relative risks if they choose to leave their case to be decided by an independent judge or jury.

Providing Equal Access for Virtual Mediations and Arbitrations: Understanding the "Digital Divide"

The "Digital Divide" identifies the gap between those who have easy and ready access to computers and the internet and those who do not. This divide has become more readily apparent during the pandemic, as individuals were pushed into their residences to "work from home" and students were similarly required to find a way to connect with their schools to "learn from home".

The divide became even more apparent within the justice system. Court appearances that switched to remote forced litigants (and even more detrimentally, criminal defendants) to find or create methods by which they could use their devices (and stay within their data plans) to ensure that they didn't miss a court date and risk dismissals of their cases, judgments against them or even the danger of bench warrants for the failure to appear.

Just as we struggle to recognize that there is food insecurity in a society that markets abundance, it is hard to accept that in the United States, there are still many who do not have computers, wi-fi access or sufficient data plans for their mobile smartphones. But it is these same individuals who are expected to simply "connect" and participate in the recently altered justice system that is attempting to carry on during a pandemic. There is a true concern over fairness in a process that is now based solely on the connectivity of the parties involved. Not only can there be a perceived bias against those who appear on a phone screen versus a computer screen but litigants who do connect remain fearful that they will be penalized or punished if their systems disconnect or their data plans run out in the middle of a court session, even while they sometimes are required to stay on "hold" for hours.

Similarly, while there has been a strong effort to move matters out of the court into alternative dispute resolution, the same obstacles exist for those seeking a remedy through private arbitrations or independent mediations. Both systems are designed for digital access. Additionally, the lack of digital access can impact one of the fundamental elements of the ADR process, that of confidentiality.

Where digital access is limited, witnesses who testify may be forced to attend proceedings using shared spaces instead of private conference rooms. Further, negotiations that might otherwise be held in private may be pushed into public areas where parties may be restricted in what they can say. Finally, with limited access to phone or computer service,, some parties may only be able to be connected sporadically rather than during an entire hearing, which can directly complicate the process.

While there may not be an easy answer to this digital access issue, recognizing the problem is a significant first step. If arbitrators and mediators are aware of the issues before the hearings and sessions begin, it will be possible to remove some of the implied bias that may come from one party being able to easily connect compared to another party who cannot. Approaching the role of third-party judge or neutral with more sensitivity to the digital access issue may create a more impartial and equitable playing field for those involved in the ADR process. Hopefully, such an open recognition of the issue can remove any stigma associated with such limited access and improve the environment needed to successfully resolve the pending dispute.

Preparing Your Clients
for Mediation

One of the most important pieces of a successful mediation is educating the parties about what a mediation is and what happens during a mediation. A lack of preparation can significantly impact the ultimate success or failure of the process.

Lawyers involved in a mediation may often forget that their clients are not familiar with the concept of mediation. They can often take for granted that their clients understand the use of alternative dispute resolution. In truth, for many parties, especially in non-commercial matters, this may be the first time that one or more of the parties has been involved in the legal process at all. It is not uncommon for some parties, who are not otherwise prepared for a mediation, to believe that mediation is simply another type of binding adjudication and that the mediator will "decide" their case for them. Oftentimes, parties can request that witnesses appear at the mediation in the expectation that they will need to present their case during the session. It is crucial for parties to understand that mediation is a non-binding process led by an independent third-party neutral who will not decide the merits of their case. Instead, the parties need to understand that mediation is an opportunity to explain their case to the other side, but neither side can be forced to resolve the dispute during the mediation and, most importantly, that the mediator is not the final decision-maker.

Similarly, parties should be told ahead of time what the lawyer's intended strategy will be during the mediation. For example, if the case involves a claim for compensation, it can be awkward for the lawyer presenting the case to make a high monetary demand during the mediation and then later attempt to persuade their client to accept a lower amount for settlement. Likewise, if a party is offering payment, it can be confusing for a lawyer to argue for a nominal amount initially and then increase that amount later in order to settle. Unless the parties involved understand and are prepared for the financial negotiation process, it may appear as if the lawyers are "giving in" or "siding" with the other party, especially if the settlement amount is significantly different from the initial demands or offers that were made. Clients can easily lose faith in their lawyers if they misunderstand the posturing that takes place during the settlement/compromise process. Again, discussing the process of mediation and the manner of negotiation with the parties in advance of the discussions can alleviate the confusion that might occur. Inherent in that preparation is an honest discussion of the value of the case. By addressing this issue in advance, the parties can be more aware of the potentials in the offers and counteroffers that are communicated to the mediator.

The parties should be prepared for the time involved in working through a mediation. Any expectation of a quick presentation and a simple discussion should be moderated before the mediation begins. Successful mediations often can take hours and, in some situations, days. The process should not be rushed for expediency. In fact, it is the time committed and exhausted by the parties involved that often lead to a successful mediation. Again, understanding that a full day may be needed for the mediation, arrangements for time off work, child-care needs, or other possible interruptions should be managed prior to starting the process.

Finally, clients should be counseled to appreciate that mediation is often the best time to resolve a dispute. It is often-times the only true period of a litigation matter during which the litigants can be in control of the resolution. Rather than turning their case over to a third-party trier of fact (judge or jury), mediation allows the parties to make their own decisions on resolution through compromise and settlement. Accordingly, counsel should also educate their respective clients on the risks and rewards of trial so that the client can weigh those elements against the offers it may make or receive.

Mediation can be a confusing concept for individuals not regularly involved in the litigation process. As such, the process should not be taken for granted. It is incumbent upon the lawyers involved in the case, those that are closest to the parties involved, to prepare the litigants for the mediation experience. Advanced preparation could make the difference between a successful or an unsuccessful ADR result.

Mediation and the Process of "Re-Thinking"

The need for mediation is conflict driven. Two or more parties with divergent interests unable to otherwise reach consensus on an issue which requires the need for third party intervention. Typically, that third party role would be filed by a judge, jury or possibly an arbitrator. But in each of those scenarios, the conflict is created by the inability to find common ground. For mediation to work, sometimes it is essential for the parties to be able to "re-think" their positions. The following are two elements of how to "re-think":

1. **Reconsider the risk of being wrong**

It is so easy to dig in with a position based on information that you are provided and the supportive opinions of others. Those assumed facts and strong beliefs can create an intractable position with little room for negotiation. But behind all that confidence of conviction, there is a risk that the facts as presented are not absolute and that the support provided is not necessarily out of certainty, but possibly out of patronage or loyalty. Parties to a dispute must accept that there is a risk that they might be wrong. The must be willing to accept new information, to consider new alternatives and new assumptions. To blindly believe that the position asserted cannot be defeated or at least tested eliminates the opportunity to be educated. It is important to remember that being wrong is not being evil or corrupt. Sometimes people are just wrong. The acceptance of that possibility, without the judgment that goes along with it, can allow the parties involved to demonstrate flexibility in their positions without acknowledging that they are somehow nefarious. Further, there is a positive quality to admitting one's mistakes. Those who can admit they are wrong and accept their missteps, maybe even find humor in the recognition of their mistakes or miscues, can personally and professionally benefit from the process of such acceptance. The willingness to be wrong can be the first significant step toward reaching the common ground needed to reach a resolution of a dispute.

2. **Separate the concept of compromise from the perception of failure**

Many of us have been raised believing in the absolutes of good and evil, right and wrong, winner and loser. Those are strong perceptions to overcome, especially in a mediation scenario where the goal is to consider compromise, to reach the "gray" between the black and white of the pending dispute. In order to reach a resolution, the parties need to reconsider the perception that to shift one's position, whether it is to accept less or to give more, is not a demonstration of weakness or of failure, but rather (especially in the context of a mediation) a demonstration of strength and a willingness to accept change. The ability to move from an assumed position of strength to a position of openness demonstrates a willingness to listen and to learn. By removing the implication of perceived failure from that act of flexibility demonstrates an attitude of compassion and tolerance which are positive attributes, not symbols of failure.

It is not an easy thing to "re-think", to break the mold of how you were taught to think or behave during your life. But in times of conflict, where emotions can escalate and differences can become accentuated, sometimes the only way to reach resolution is to break those structures of belief, to question yourself and those around you. To reconsider the risk of what it means to be wrong and what it means to compromise.

Addressing the Issue of Impartiality and Bias in Mediations

A mediator, by definition, must be an independent, unbiased, impartial participant in the negotiation process to help the disputing parties reach a resolution of their dispute. That independence from the parties and their advocates is a crucial element of the process, since it allows the participants to feel confident that the mediator is honest in his/her contribution to the process and will not be swayed by any undisclosed circumstances.

This issue of mediator "independence" or "neutrality" can therefore be a factor in the initial selection of the mediator. Many times, the mediator has been used previously by one lawyer or the other, there may in fact be a former personal or professional relationship with the mediator which leads to their introduction. Commonly, it is this "past" experience with the mediator that elevates the mediator's recommendation as a "strong" mediator, a "good" listener or an "effective" neutral.

So then how can a mediator, who may have a history with one lawyer, prove their ability to play a successful, yet neutral, role in the mediation? The answer involves full disclosure. A potential mediator must be as transparent as possible when notifying all participants of their past history and connections with the parties and their counsel. While a mediator is different from an arbitrator who is left to ultimately make a binding decision against one party or the other, the same transparency is a vital piece in the selection and approval of a mediator. No party or counsel wants to learn later that the mediator in the room may have a connection to the other side that was insufficiently disclosed. Therefore, full disclosure is the first step in creating a positive and fair mediation process.

The Uniform Mediation Act, recently enacted in Georgia, addresses this disclosure obligation within the statute as follows:

OCGA § 9-17-8 [Qualifications of mediator; impartiality]

(a) Before accepting a mediation, an individual who is requested to serve as a mediator shall:

(1) Make an inquiry that is reasonable under the circumstances to determine whether there are any known facts that a reasonable individual would consider likely to affect the impartiality of the mediator, including a financial or personal interest in the outcome of the mediation and an existing or past relationship with a mediation party or foreseeable participant in the mediation; and **(2)** Disclose any such known fact to the mediation parties as soon as is practical before accepting a mediation.

(b) If a mediator learns any fact described in paragraph (1) of subsection (a) of this Code section after accepting a mediation, the mediator shall disclose it as soon as is practicable.

(c) At the request of a mediation party, an individual who is requested to serve as a mediator shall disclose the mediator's qualifications to mediate a dispute.

(d) A person that violates subsection (a) or (b) of this Code section is precluded by the violation from asserting a privilege under Code Section 9-17-3.

(e) Subsection (a), (b), or (c) of this Code section shall not apply to an individual acting as a judge.

(f) This chapter shall not require that a mediator have a special qualification by background or profession.

Mediators' services are best used to help the parties find, under their own analysis, a method for the resolution of a dispute. To avoid any appearance of bias, a mediator should motivate, not manipulate, the parties to reach their common resolution. Although mediators can assist the process by being evaluative, they must clarify their opinions based on their perspective and background. Mediators can suggest, but not impose their opinions or recommendations. A successful mediator must understand the risk of bias impacting the mediation process and with such recognition, work to avoid any influence in the negotiation process. A mediator who fails to acknowledge the risk of bias in the mediation is not acknowledging a realistic element of the process.

Bottom line, neutrality is one of the bedrocks of a fair and impartial mediation process. Any issues that threaten that impartiality can destroy the opportunity for a successful mediation. Disclosure and honest discussions on the topic of bias can help avoid potential problems relating to the perception of fairness and lead the parties to a successful resolution of their dispute.

Should Mediation Fall within the "Standard of Care" for Lawyers Representing Litigants?

In that the American Arbitration Association reports an 85% success rate for mediations leading to the settlement of disputes (apparently consistent with other institutional alternative dispute resolution providers), the following question should be considered. Should participation in a mediation be included within a lawyer's standard or duty of care to its clients when representing litigants in a dispute? In other words, rather than considering mediation only as an alternative to dispute resolution, should it be required?

The Courts, both federal and state, have considered this issue. Many of them recognize the success of mediation as a method for resolving disputes, thereby reducing their backlogged dockets. As a result, numerous judiciaries now mandate mediation as a pre-trial condition. But absent a court directive, should counsel be required to participate in a mediation in all of its litigation matters, as part of the lawyer's ethical duty, or standard of care to its clients?

This issue has received increased attention during the Covid pandemic when courts in many jurisdictions were closed and trials were delayed. Civil litigants who previously may have expected their trials to be scheduled within a year are now waiting more than two years for their cases to be heard. Should counsel for the parties, both Plaintiffs and Defendants, be obligated to participate in mediation in order to ease the burden on our judicial system?

Keep in mind, mediation is non-binding and no one can force parties to settle during the mediation process. Ultimately, this control that the litigants have in the mediation process may, indeed, be its strongest attribute. The fact that only the litigants themselves can determine the outcome of the mediation is a unique characteristic of the process. And while simply requiring both sides to sit in a room together, even with a qualified mediator, will not always lead to a peaceful resolution of the dispute, it begs the question - should the parties be required to at least try, given that the success rate is typically high if the parties, in good faith, at least attempt to discuss resolution?

Every case is different and the reality is that mediation, even with its strengths, is not always the right solution. If mediation is to be required, or even considered, as part of a lawyer's "standard of care" for its clients, how would that standard be measured? By the success or failure of the mediation itself? And if required, at what point in the litigation process should mediation be attempted? Is it too early to mediate before discovery has been completed and not all facts are known? Is it too late to mediate right before trial, when the parties have potentially "dug-in" to their positions?

That said, these are unusual times. Our judicial system is clearly reeling from the impacts of the pandemic. Civil litigants who are seeking a remedy for their alleged wrongs, or those who are defending their positions, are entitled to seek closure. This may be the best time for mediation to move from its current position as an *alternative* for dispute resolution to becoming an *obligation* for dispute resolution.

Creative Thinking in Mediations

The black robed judge peered over the elevated large wooden bench and spoke to the litigants with a stern tone. "I'm suggesting that the parties attempt to mediate their dispute. Why? Because all I can do from the bench is issue a money judgment either for or against one of the parties. But in mediation you have the control to work out a resolution that offers relief beyond money. You can transfer property, make payment plans, and be as creative as you need to be to resolve your dispute. I think your case can be best handled with this approach." The parties nodded in agreement and thanked the Judge for the referral. "Send me some names" one of the lawyers said to the other as he packed up his briefcase. "Put your thinking cap on" the other answered with a grin. Then he added "we'll need to get creative to get this case settled before trial!"

Although fictionalized, it is this approach to alternative dispute resolution that distinguishes mediation from the linear results that can be found by litigating cases in court. Judges are limited for the most part in offering any decisions beyond the awarding of money judgments to the litigating parties. Mediation provides an open whiteboard of options for the parties to resolve their dispute. Often times, the issue may simply be the amount of time that one party needs to pay its debts. Sometimes, it's the simple apology that is needed to initiate closure. And certainly, there are times where all that is truly needed is for the litigants to have the opportunity to express themselves in front of the other party, to literally feel as if they have "had their day in court" before they can begin to accept the possibility of a negotiated resolution.

A skilled mediator can use this creative thinking to help settle cases that typically would be pushed to impasse. By looking "outside of the money" and asking what the parties are really looking for to reach satisfaction in their dispute, a mediator may be able to identify non-monetary solutions to the dispute. So instead of two companies fighting over a product delivery that went bad and now losing that customer forever in a payment dispute, maybe mediation can create a "do-over" opportunity to re-establish that business relationship for future sales. There is no end to how adversarial parties can work together to find business solutions to their disputes when given the opportunity. Again, this type of opportunity for creative solutions in not present in the courtroom like it is in the private venue of mediation.

Additionally, changing a litigant's viewpoint in settlement discussions from thinking about what may be "lost" in settlement as compared to what may be "gained" in settlement is also an effective tool for a mediator.

And the list of things that can be gained by settlement rather than through extended litigation is virtually endless. To start, the parties can think about the possibility of healing the broken relationship between the warring parties. Maybe the parties started off as friends, or maybe the two companies now involved in a dispute previously had a long-standing relationship. Mediation can help mend those relationships where lengthy litigation can only lead to further acrimony and animosity. And there is also the cost of litigation. These days the cost of battling a case in court, with extended docket delays and intrusive discovery methods, may end up bankrupting a company before the litigation can be completed. And there is, of course, the mental toll taken upon people and companies involved in long term litigation. Lawsuits can be very stressful and can distract business owners away from their main goal of growing their business. There sometimes can be nothing more devastating to a business then a pending lawsuit that draws time, energy and attention away from operating that business.

Or maybe it's simply that the public nature of a trial may impact customer attitudes which might hurt company sales. There seems to be much to gain by resolving a case privately rather than risking ongoing public attention to the dispute. Clearly, the private nature of mediation compared to a public trial can be a significant benefit when looking at considerations for settlement. And finally, settlements create true closure to disputes whereas litigation in court may only result in lengthy appeals before reaching a final resolution.

Mediators need to help the parties consider all of these factors when measuring what settlements may be worth in the long run. This type of creative thinking can lead to open dialogue and beneficial movement toward mutual dispute resolution.

Confidentiality in Mediation: Creating a Safe Space

A cornerstone of mediation as an approach towards dispute resolution is the understanding that the process is considered confidential. Why is this important? Essentially, it is the fact that the parties can freely discuss the merits of their case, without the fear that their position will be undermined, that permit the mediation process to help parties ultimately settle their claims. In that the mediation process is confidential and the environment in which the discussions are held are therefore considered safe, create the opportunity for parties to honestly address their underlying motivations regarding the dispute, their anxieties regarding their risks and their considerations for settlement. Without a comfort of such confidentiality regarding those discussions, mediation would cease to be an effective tool for dispute resolution.

It is important to understand the context for why these mediations discussions are confidential. Certainly, the easiest way to approach this issue is recognizing that in both under federal and state law settlement discussions between parties are protected communications. Certainly, as the law understands and supports, parties in a dispute would never entertain settlement or compromise discussions if those conversations were admissible and could be used against them to demonstrate weakness in their claims or demands. As such, these communications, once identified as such, essentially remain privileged in order to motivate parties to participate in open dialogue for resolution without the fear of illustrating any offers to a judge or jury as an admission regarding the relative strength or weakness of that party's case.

The same logic applies to the confidentiality that exists in the mediation process and is a central ingredient in the trust relationship that is developed between the mediator and the participating parties. It is only by a party believing that not only is their effort at compromise confidential, but that their discussions with the mediator are confidential, that a party can recognize and freely accept the inevitable reality that lawsuits are expensive, time consuming, emotionally challenging and, ultimately, come with no guarantees of success. Once those honest elements are considered, again with the protection of confidentiality, can parties truly move towards the necessary steps of potential resolution.

The best starting point to establish that comfort of confidentiality is in the mediation agreement itself. It is within the terms of that agreement where the parties can acknowledge and agree that their discussions will remain confidential, including the restriction against calling the mediator as a witness in any proceeding arising from the mediation. The mediation agreement should highlight as well that the confidentiality shall extend outside of the mediation itself, especially in those circumstances where a settlement is not reached during the mediation and the mediator continues to facilitate discussions with the parties afterwards.

In addition to the confidentiality within the mediation process itself is the specific issues of confidentiality that arise during caucus discussions which occur only between one party and the mediator. Generally, it is understood that these conversations themselves are confidential, unless permission is given by the party for the mediator to disclose certain elements of the conversation. Sometimes these shared bits of information that are carried by the mediator between the parties can be the key points that help motivate the resolution of a case. Again, the sense of trustworthiness between the parties and the mediator can permit a higher level of open dialogue. Often times it is the comfort of confidentiality where a party, otherwise stagnant in their resolve about their position in a case, can feel free to be more flexible and creative in order to reach a solution to the conflict.

Certainly, there are exceptions to this shield of confidentiality in mediations. Although generally conversations and information disclosed during mediations are privileged, the confidentiality protections do not apply if a party makes a threat against another party or person concerning physical harm or property damage, or if information concerning the commission of a crime. Additionally, the confidentiality can be waived if a claim is asserted by a party against a mediator alleging professional misconduct. In such a case the mediator reserves the right to defend itself by relying on information provided during the mediation process that otherwise would remain confidential.

At the end of the day, mediation as an alternative dispute resolution process can only work when the parties participate in good faith and come to the mediation to seek common ground. The shield or privilege of confidentiality during the process absolutely contributes to the potential success of the endeavor. A mediator that offers the comfort and trust of this confidential process will inevitably succeed as compared to a mediation environment where such a safe space has not been created.

Corporate In-House Mediation Programs

Employment disputes inside corporations are inevitable. Even with strong human resource oversight, companies cannot avoid the likelihood of claims arising from their employees, whether they are wage related or rise to the level of discrimination or ADA violations.

Due to the increased cost of court litigation, many companies have turned to offering in-house alternative dispute resolution options. Many companies believe that this solution can create a better and more positive forum to handle employment claims at earlier stages, with a positive tone toward resolution. Such an attitude can avoid long, drawn-out court battles that often result in financial impacts to the companies involved.

An in-house ADR program can present an initial option for non-binding mediation, to be administered either by an in-house staff mediator or an outside provider who is familiar with the policies of the company involved as well as the relevant employment law at issue in the dispute. An outside provider can be, and usually is, an attorney, but certainly there are mediators who are not attorneys that have the training needed to facilitate the ADR process.

It is thought that by having these in-house programs available, employees are more comfortable bringing an issue to light as compared to letting the matter fester. Again, early communication and possible resolution of a dispute on the early side may help avoid a larger issue down the road if not addressed. Further, if a supervisor or manager is responsible for improper actions, the issues may only affect one employee initially, but later, if not addressed, could later involve multiple employees.

Generally these in-house ADR programs start with an offer at non-binding mediation and, if not resolved, the option can then include binding arbitration. These options, since they are in-house, can limit the expense involved to the company, especially since the law often requires the company, not the employee, to pay for the mediator or arbitrator's time and expenses.

Certainly, the culture of offering such a resolution program is crucial to its success. Employees should be encouraged to come forward with their disputes and there should be significant penalties against anyone who retaliates against an employee who brings a claim. A company may decide to make these ADR programs required as part of their employment rules. The Courts have generally upheld an employer's rights to require ADR if it is part of an employee's contract or handbook. Other companies simply offer ADR as an option, without making it mandatory. In such a case, an employee may be more willing to participate instead of believing that the process is required and possibly "rigged".

Since in-house ADR mediation and arbitration programs are not new, there is considerable data available to demonstrate its success. And even though many of the companies that utilize these programs are larger, even smaller companies should consider implementing this approach to workplace dispute resolution. Again, the cost in the long run is far lower than disputes which exist in the court and involve long term discovery, extensive trial time and possible appeals.

The Advantages of a Dispute Resolution Board

One of the programs that has developed from the growing evolution of alternative dispute resolution is that of Dispute Resolution Boards.

A Dispute Resolution Board or "DRB" is a panel of independent, neutral professionals typically used in large construction projects to encourage not only the avoidance or prevention of disputes during the project but, if needed, to assist in the resolution of disputes that may arise during the project. Those who work in the construction industry are patently aware of the constant conflicts that may arise between the multiple parties working concurrently on a project. These DRB's are created to diffuse any issues that arise thereby keeping the project on schedule.

An often-used approach for creating a Dispute Resolution Board is for an Owner and General Contractor to each choose a participant for the panel and then for those two panelists to select a third member. For smaller projects, to avoid excessive costs, the Owner and General Contractor will simply jointly select a third-party neutral to manage the dispute process.

The decision to rely on a DRB, whether a single individual or a panel, is typically successful one, because that third-party decision maker is committed to being involved in the project from the beginning to the end. Since this third party is an essential participant in the project, DRB members are invested in the project from the beginning and therefore are acquainted with the project from the start. As disputes arise, there is no time lost having to familiarize a third party with the facts of the project. The DRB can get to the heart of the dispute quickly.

As a neutral, independent participant, a DRB panelist can provide help to impacted parties so they can reach a resolution of any issues that cannot otherwise be easily settled during the project. This reliance on an impartial person or panel of professionals to manage any problem-solving during a project can help to move that project forward when needed.

The use of DRB's can hopefully create a less adversarial environment on the related project. When viewed in a preventative light, DRB's have helped project participants avoid the need for litigation. DRB's allow all parties in the project to participate in the resolution process. No alienation of the subcontractors, architects or suppliers occurs. All parties are vested with a global interest in creating a successful project without the initiation of disputes. Therefore, the decision to utilize a

DRB on a project can help avoid or minimize disputes, prevent any disputes that do arise from lingering on a project, and ultimately assist in avoiding project delays caused by disputes as well as the cost impact those disputes have on the project.

Oftentimes a DRB can assist with "real-time" resolutions of matters as they arise. DRB's can be vested by agreement with the power to make recommendations on how to resolve disputes or they can be appointed by contract with the power to make binding decisions. Typically, most DRB's are contractually provided with the right to make non-binding, admissible recommendations with an understanding that, if not resolved, the dispute may then be carried over, with or without counsel, to a later binding process, whether that is through arbitration or the courts.

Is There a Place for Collaborative Law in the Resolution of Commercial Disputes?

The concept of "collaborative law" as a means of resolving disputes without going to court has been utilized within the family law community for years. When applied in domestic and custody cases, the spouses voluntarily agree to make a good faith effort to resolve their disputes without judicial intervention and further agree to support their efforts with outside experts (financial and psychological) if or when needed. Such a collaborative approach is then formalized contractually in a "participation agreement" where the parties not only accept to make their best efforts to compromise and settle but also commit to the notion that, if their efforts to collaborate fail, the attorneys representing each side will be disqualified from representing the parties in court. Since the parties are willing to attempt this collaborative process, before filing any action in court, the joint willingness to participate creates an implied alignment of goals.

Further, these participation agreements outline issues such as confidentiality of communications, privileged work product of lawyers and outside experts and the alternative use of mediation and arbitration for dispute resolution. But most importantly, the use of this collaborative law approach represents a sincere desire by the parties involved to do whatever they can to work out their differences without the cost, expense, and personal impact caused by going to court to resolve their dispute. A final piece of the collaborative law system is that it remains voluntary throughout the process. Therefore, participants can, at any time, terminate the process and divert the matter to a court or tribunal to litigate their dispute.

Since this resolution method works so well in domestic matters, it seems like there should be obvious applications for this process in other civil and commercial disputes. All it would take is a commitment from practitioners to accept the idea that, under collaborative law theory, if the lawyers involved in the collaborative process fail to resolve the dispute, they will withdraw from their representation of the participating parties. Apart from that, most everything else in a standard collaborative law participation agreement follows the general conditions of any other representation agreement, including the protections related to confidential communications, lack of admissibility as evidence and work product privilege (subject to exceptions for personal injury or criminal activity).

More than twenty states have enacted some form of the "Uniform Collaborative Law Act" as recommended by the Uniform Law Commission. The opportunity for a greater acceptance and utilization of collaborative law in general civil litigation matters should be at the forefront for ADR professionals and practitioners, all of whom support the need for creative methods to help their clients reach resolutions of civil disputes without the need for court.

Understanding Settlement Brackets

If there is but one job for a mediator, it is to keep the disputing parties talking. As long as there is communication and energy about the possibility of settling a dispute, then there is hope for a resolution. Often times talk of adding "bracketing" to the discussion occurs simply for that reason... another way to keep the parties talking where other efforts may have failed. Compared to typical high/low negotiations, bracketing can re-energize the parties and help focus them in on what might be a more manageable difference between their positions.

So how does it work? Instead of going back and forth with standard offers from distant positions, a bracket presents a jump for the parties to work within a narrower band of discussion. The best analogy to offer is that of a football field. Instead of each side working from their own ten-yard lines (therefore being eighty yards apart), the parties agree that if one side moves to the forty-yard line the other side will also move to their forty-yard line. In such an instance, their positions are now only twenty yards apart. It doesn't necessarily mean that they will meet in the middle of the field, but now the differential is much smaller and more workable. From a mediator's perspective, such a move is significant and instrumental in helping the parties reach an ultimate resolution of their dispute.

A negative connotation associated with bracketing is that it forces the two parties to "meet in the middle" or implies that they will do so. That is not the case. Ultimately the purpose of bracketing is to accelerate the parties' movement into that smaller playing field. Where the ball ultimately ends up still depends on the willingness of the parties to move their offers closer. But now instead of being eighty yards apart, where frustration can creep into the process, the parties are now only twenty yards apart and a sense or possibility can fill the room.

Sometimes there can be two brackets put forward, with each side offering something different. In such a case the same advantages exist, it just may require the mediator to present both brackets simultaneously to find a common overlap. But bracketing need not be a mathematical exercise to calculate midpoints between the parties. Instead, it should be seen as a psychological exercise for the parties demonstrating a willingness to move from a possible stalemate position to a new one. Any such movement in a settlement discussion can be deemed a success.

Ultimately, bracketing is a matter of trust. It must be offered as a promise for each side to commit to the move. The success of bracketing is the fact that the movement by one side is conditioned upon the fulfillment of the promise by the other side. Once that occurs, the mediator should be able to help the parties, now working from a shorter distance apart, to find a place where both sides can be satisfied with their settlement.

Mediating with Subject Matter Experts

Mediation, as a method of alternative dispute resolution, continues to be an evolving art. Mediators study the psychology of body language, the use of settlement brackets and the leverage of the rising cost of litigation, all to help parties reach a resolution of their disputes without the stress, time and cost of trials. The ranks of mediators are increasing, as experienced lawyers and often retired judges step into the arena of ADR to use their skills to help settle pending cases. Even non-lawyers are participating as mediators, especially if their particular employment experiences have guided them into the field of collaborative conflict resolution (for example in the areas of human resources/employment or engineering/construction).

As the process and methodology of successful mediations have grown and expanded, mediators who are knowledgeable and experienced in a particular subject matter area of law might be crucial to assist disputing parties in reaching a resolution of their case. Many times, the more a mediator knows and understands a particular area of law, the more helpful the mediator can be in guiding the parties toward an understanding of the value of a party-controlled settlement when compared a judge or jury decision made outside the authority of the impacted parties.

The value and growth of "subject matter experts" as mediators has been measurable over the last few years. The selection of a specific mediator can oftentimes be a crucial element in reaching any potential closure during the mediation process. The selection of a mediator who has either tried cases in the area of law, has adjudicated cases in that field or has worked as a non-lawyer in that trade, may all enhance the ability of the mediator to assist the parties in finding areas of conciliation and closure that may otherwise not occur without the guidance of the specialized mediator.

Of course, sometimes nothing can beat a skilled general mediator. Subject matter experts can sometimes miss the subtle behaviors and expectations that are needed to reach settlements, while an experienced mediator can decipher these without significant effort. For all of the focus on what the law might say on any particular topic, sometimes settlements rise or fall on the more subjective issues that face the parties. In those cases, the general skill, compassion and personality of the third-party neutral may be more important than the specific background of the mediator. At the end of the day, all of these issues need to be weighed when the parties select a mediator to help them with their case. Nevertheless, as the world of mediation grows and parties are given endless choices of mediators, subject matter knowledge cannot be ignored as one of the essential pieces that may be needed to have a successful mediation.

The Benefits of
Pre-Litigation Mediation

If the whole purpose of mediation is to allow the parties to reach a self-controlled resolution of their dispute without the cost and expense of litigation, the obvious question is why do most mediations occur long after the case has started, and the parties have inevitably become more entrenched in their positions?

If alternative dispute resolution is really meant to offer a cost effective and positive methodology to resolve disputes out of the court system, it seems that the warring parties might be better off taking their dispute before a third-party neutral at the beginning of their conflict rather than after the fight has started.

Although doubters might argue that pre-litigation dispute resolution risks a settlement without knowledge of all of the relevant facts that would be obtained from discovery, advocates would otherwise suggest that extended discovery is not always helpful in clarifying the respective positions of opposing parties. Certainly, in particular cases with conflicting facts, extended discovery may not even help to verify incongruent facts or validate liability claims. It is in these cases, where discovery may not be necessarily or especially constructive, that pre-litigation mediation might be the best solution.

Here are a few suggestions for parties pursuing pre-litigation mediation. First, an agreement addressing absolute confidentiality is key. Agreeing to confidential and inadmissible settlement negotiations in advance of filing a lawsuit is crucial to allowing an open and honest exchange of communication for settlement. Tantamount to the potential success of pre-litigation mediation is the uniform and collective understanding that any offers made, or even admissions conceded, cannot be used against the parties later if the case cannot be resolved.

Within that same context, whereas pre-mediation statements are often created only for the mediator's review prior to the mediation itself, in pre-litigation mediation it is recommended that the parties directly share their pre-mediation statements with each other. For a true chance for settlement, the disputing parties are encouraged to "lay all the cards on the table" in these pre-mediation statements so that all facts and legal authorities are disclosed which would allow the affected parties the greatest opportunity to evaluate their potential risks if the claims and counterclaims were to proceed to litigation.

The other consideration for pre-litigation mediation is the reality that, once in litigation, parties are more likely to become further entrenched in their positions over time due to the emotion involved. The litigation process can increase the negative perspectives of the parties and make the dispute worse than when it started. When emotions overtake logic, bringing long-term disputing parties together in the same room for settlement discussions can become impossible. One way to avoid this emotional obstacle is to seek mediation early before that positioning occurs.

For an individual claimant, pre-litigation mediation offers a quick resolution, maintenance of the emotional costs associated with litigation and a potential return to normalcy more quickly than long-term litigation. From a business perspective, the certainty and finality of a mediated result can be extremely valuable. Often for companies the opportunity to settle can create a cap for the potential losses that might otherwise affect a business' credit rating and insurability (or cost of insurance). Additionally, an early settlement can reduce the possibility of negative publicity that could affect the reputation of a business involved in a public litigation matter.

Lastly, regardless of the parties' perspective on their success at trial, nothing is for certain in court. Even a party that has prevailed can sometimes lose its case on later appeals. If the parties can "self-control" their outcomes, the resolution is often better, quicker and more positive than the results obtained after years of litigation.

At the end of the day, pre-litigation mediation should remain an available option for disputing parties in every case. Although parties may choose to utilize ADR later in the litigation process, based on the facts and issues presented, pre-litigation mediation might be a positive strategy for the parties to consider and a worthy topic to discuss.

What is "Impartiality" for a Mediator?

One of the most important tenets or rules for a mediator is to remain impartial to the parties engaged in a dispute during the course of the mediation process. The acceptance of the mediator as a true "neutral" is essential to assisting the parties in recognizing and accepting their risks in the litigation process and appreciating the benefits of reaching a mutual resolution and settlement of their dispute.

But what is impartiality? It is defined as being "fair", "objective" and in some instances "detached" from the issues under debate. Therefore, to be an impartial mediator, there is an inherent separateness between the mediator who is facilitating the negotiation and the parties that will be impacted by the potential resolution.

How far must this question of impartiality extend? Often, the first time this issue arises is in the selection of the mediator. So, is it appropriate to select a mediator who is familiar with one party or one counsel over the other? A mediator can still be effective even if well known by a party or connected professionally to counsel. But a mediator should absolutely disclose all such connections and relationships before the mediation so that the involved parties and counsel can evaluate the relationships and judge the potential impact on fairness of the process. Any and all conflicts of interest must be avoided and disclosed to all parties and counsel involved.

Once a mediator is selected, the issue of impartiality could next arise during the mediation itself. As a neutral, the mediator does not have the authority to render any decisions between the parties. However, that might not matter if either party believes that the mediator's alliances have shifted toward one party over the other or that the mediator's neutrality has been compromised.

If, at any time, the mediator believes that there is a developing conflict or any bias between the mediator and any of the parties involved, it is best that the mediator withdraw itself from the mediation, rather than cast doubt on the integrity of the mediation process. Otherwise, a mediator can proceed with the mediation unless and until any party or counsel objects to their continuing service. A mediator must withdraw if requested by the parties or their counsel.

A mediator should do its best to maintain all appearances of neutrality. The most a mediator can do is assist the parties in recognizing the risks of continuing litigation and the benefits of self-determination in finding settlement and closure. It is not the easiest job for a mediator to remain impartial if a mediator struggles in its interactions with one party over another. But at the end of the day, a mediator's fairness and neutrality are what make the mediator one of the most helpful participants in the process. If that independence is lost, the integrity and success of the process can fail.

In Mediation, Attitude is Everything!

To reach any resolution in the midst of conflict, the intentionality of the process is necessary. All parties involved in the dispute must be interested in reaching a settlement and must be invested in the effort to do so. No one should be forced to settle their dispute. But it is likely impossible to actually reach a resolution unless there is a willingness to try.

Some court ordered mediations are frequently unsuccessful because the parties involved are not in the mindset at the time to discuss settlement. A court order to participate in mediation is often not as meaningful as the parties independently reaching a point in the dispute process where the parties themselves agree that mediation might be helpful. Many court-ordered mediations are ultimately successful because, even if the parties don't initially seek a resolution, often times once they are in the process, they can recognize the benefit of the discussions and the possibility of seeking closure of their dispute.

But whether court-ordered or voluntary, if parties to a mediation are going to reach a settlement, the attitude they bring to the process is extremely important. If the parties are not in a frame of mind to listen, learn and consider both the costs and benefits of continuing their lawsuit, a settlement is unlikely.

So how can a mediator motivate the parties involved to participate with a positive attitude? Whether the case involves a personal matter or a business issue, one of the values of mediation is that it is a non-binding process. So, what is there to lose? Nothing. In fact, in many ways the worst thing that might happen following a mediation is that the parties end up exactly where they started before the mediation - in a lawsuit. But the result of the mediation might also be the resolution of the action. In fact, simply participating in a mediation could allow the parties to recognize their reality of engaging in a litigation process, both as to the time and expense involved with a lawsuit but also, and sometimes more importantly, the emotional currency expended in such a fight.

Once a party realizes there is nothing to lose and that they are in control of what happens during the mediation process, hopefully the party's attitude about engaging in the process will change as well. If a party's viewpoint is positive (engaging in an act without risk) then that outlook might change the overall result of the party's effort during the mediation process. Again, approaching mediation without an open and optimistic attitude will only make the potential of resolution that much more difficult to achieve.

Successful Mediations and
the Power of Listening

One of my favorite expressions has always been "we have two ears and one mouth so that we can listen twice as much as we speak." This adage may be nowhere more important than during a mediation. Ultimately, in a setting where all sides have come in good faith to seek a resolution of their dispute, the importance of listening and the psychological and physical elements of true listening are crucial to support the possible success of the mediation process.

The concept of listening comes with many elements. Certainly, one of those features is the focus and attention given to the party talking. Obviously, if one person is talking and the other side is interrupting or is distracted by extraneous factors (such as a smartphone), the person talking might believe their comments are not honestly being heard or considered. Without the trust that the party listening is paying attention to what is being said, the credibility of the conversation is weakened. This is one of the reasons why the effort to create eye contact between the speaker and the listener is important. Certainly, if the parties fail to establish any eye contact during their communication, the speaker might assume that the listener cannot be swayed, is bored or, possibly, that the listener is suffering some guilt or shame regarding the matter being discussed.

Just as true attention is important during a conversation, the clarity of the content of that conversation is equally salient. Although interruptions may not be appropriate during the conversation itself, it is critically important in the process of listening to make sure the message being conveyed is clear and understood by the party who is listening. The speaker should not assume that what they are saying is absolutely clear to the listener. Therefore, after the speaker is finished, time set aside for questions can be very helpful to the process. If the listener doesn't understand statements that are made, it is not a demonstration of weakness to ask questions. In fact, such questions may actually be very helpful in clearing up issues for both sides.

Additionally, another part of listening or "hearing" the other side during a discussion of resolution is the need to maintain an open mind to the facts and law that relate to the dispute between the parties. Such openness in communication can create a connection between the parties, which may engender empathy toward the other side involved in a dispute. Any such affinity towards an adversary in a dispute may be a necessary element towards reaching a resolution.

Finally, every part of a conversation includes not only what the person says, but how they say it. The physical part of any conversation is a true validation of the person's intent in what they are saying whether the words are said with open arms and a smile compared to crossed arms and closed eyes. To have effective communications the parties, notwithstanding their position in the dispute, must make a good faith effort to restrain from aggressive behavior or any demonstration of disregard for the comments that are being made. Even though an opposing party may disagree with what is being said, the willingness to listen, without interruption, and without physical barriers, may lead towards a connection that can bridge the gap in an existing dispute.

Resolving Employment
Disputes In-House

The success of mediation is well known. In excess of 85% of all cases are settled when the parties come together to talk about their dispute, when each side has the opportunity to be heard and, most importantly, take an active role in crafting a resolution to the pending dispute. What is often noted by judges that assign their cases to mediation is that "mediation gives the parties the ability to control the conclusion of their dispute. Once the dispute goes to court, all decisions are left to the judge or jury and the parties no longer have any control over the outcome."

But often the mediation process is only considered after the lawsuit has been filed, after discovery has been conducted and the parties are on the "courthouse steps" prepared for trial. By then the parties have likely spent a great deal of money, have personally invested much time and energy in the matter and unfortunately, may have hardened their respective positions as a result of the acrimony and animosity that often accompanies lawsuits.

Therefore, the movement recently has been to consider alternative dispute resolution on the front end of a claim after it occurs, before too much time and money has been spent. This approach works extremely well in the employment world, where employees may seek a remedy as a result of a poor evaluation, an altercation with management, a firing or a claim of harassment. If a system is in place for the employee to address their concerns and possibly even resolve them early, all sides are deemed to be better off. From a company bottom line perspective, the ability to resolve an employee claim through in-house dispute resolution significantly reduces the amount of money spent by the company in litigation, reduces overall insurance costs and also reduces the cost of settlement since many times the resolution is not limited to the payment of money but may involve instead letters of recommendation, a withdrawal of an objection to unemployment compensation, the creation of an accommodation for a disabled employee or even a re-hire.

So how would a company go about starting an in-house dispute resolution program? Initially, it all would flow from a "dispute plan" being included as part of the company's employee handbook. The handbook would provide for different levels of addressing an employee's complaint, from notification to a supervisor to a referral to upper management to even the option of using an employee peer review method to evaluate the complaint. But ultimately, if those initial internal systems don't lead to a solution, the matter would then be referred to a mediator who is paid for by the company but independent and unbiased. The employee would be able to choose from a list of qualified mediators who have knowledge and experience in the claims at issue. The mediation would be deemed as "non-binding" meaning that the parties who come together are not required to reach a resolution of their dispute nor will the selected mediator make a decision or render a verdict about the parties' dispute. If the matter can't be resolved, then there is no impact to the parties' respective claims or positions. However, if a settlement is reached and an agreement of terms is prepared, that settlement can then be binding on the parties as a means to create a conclusion to the ongoing dispute.

For this mediation approach to be successful, it would need to be included in the company's employment handbook as a pre-condition to the filing of any action by the employee against the company. For example, there could be language in the employment handbook (under claims and disputes) which could read as follows:

Any controversy, claim or dispute arising out of the employee's employment with the company shall first be brought to the supervisor or managers responsible for that employee and if needed, to officers of the company that are responsible for HR matters. If the claim, controversy or dispute cannot be settled internally through this process, then prior to the filing of any legal claim against the Company, the employee agrees to first participate in a mediation led by an independent, third party neutral. A list of approved mediators will be provided to the employee upon request and any

***such mediator may be selected by the employee
to conduct the mediation.***

Conflicts are inevitable. Certainly, even as litigious as
our society has become, not every conflict needs to
become a lawsuit. With early intervention, especially in
the workplace, resolution can not only have a beneficial
financial impact for the parties, but an atmosphere of
dispute resolution can also transform a workplace
environment into one where an employee can see that
their complaint is being heard, can become a mutual
participant in the solution to the problem and can also
share in the rebuilding of the impacted employment
relationship. All of those features create a positive
energy to the resolution process as compared to
the inevitable negative energy that flows from being
adversarial litigants in a lawsuit.

Creating Constructive Ideas
to Reach a Solution

One of the unique benefits of participating in a mediation is opening the door and allowing another voice to enter the room. Litigants and their counsel will readily admit that after protracted litigation and the ongoing acrimony that often escalates within a dispute, it is oftentimes very difficult for the parties involved to manage their own direct negotiations to reach a resolution of the case. After time, positions are often intractable, opinions intransigent and compromise unattainable. Mediation offers the unique opportunity to invite an un-bias participant into the situation, giving that person the chance to invite a new perspective, a new mindset and a new attitude into the discussion.

A good mediator is an impartial contributor who listens to all sides, is non-threatening in their inquiries and is unprejudiced in their reactions. A good mediator is one who not only shuttles offers between otherwise non-communicative or non-receptive parties but a person who seeks to find constructive alternatives between them to reach a resolution.

Since the lawyers involved in disputes are typically stuck to their positions, or limited due to their advocacy to narrow demands, a third-party mediator has the flexibility, without losing credibility or strength, to sometimes offer unusual suggestions to reach compromise. It is oftentimes this "out of the box" approach that can spark a pathway to new discussions or a recommendation that might ultimately lead to a solution. Whether the deliberation involves payment plans, compensation through business credits, waivers of medical liens, an agreement to manage out of date warranty repairs or a litany of other creative approaches, participating in a mediation may be the best way for the parties to allow themselves a mechanism towards open dialogue and fresh perspectives.

It is in that mind-set that parties to a mediation should welcome the involvement of an intermediary. Not as a person who will solely referee the dispute before them but as a person who is encouraged to search the parties to determine their ultimate goals that are internal to the dispute. This is one of the reasons why good mediators also need to be good listeners, because those goals are often disguised behind the bitterness and rancor that springs from litigation.

Certainly, many disputes offer cut and dried solutions. But it is in those cases where the parties fail to connect that mediation can oftentimes be the best method toward solution. Allowing the parties to consider all options, even creative ones, to control the settlement of their own dispute before a judge or jury needs to, is one of the best qualities of mediation and one of the best reasons to consider alternative dispute resolution.

What is the "Mediation Privilege"?

Much has been discussed over the years as to the importance of maintaining the concept of confidentiality as part of the mediation process. Any concern relating to lack of confidentiality during the process would risk the incentive of openness and honesty during settlement discussions. In that the concept of confidentiality is crucial for a successful mediation, it is helpful to dig deeper toward clarifying specific protections that should be included within a mediation agreement. Guiding that clarity are the rules provided within the Uniform Mediation Act, which has been incorporated by a dozen states throughout the Country. The UMA addresses some clear points as to what confidentiality readily means as to the parties, non-parties, lawyers and the mediator itself. The guideposts for what could be described as a "Mediation Privilege" are outlined under Sections 4, 5 and 6 of the UMA and are worth closer consideration and review.

SECTION 4. PRIVILEGE AGAINST DISCLOSURE; ADMISSIBILITY; DISCOVERY.

(a) Except as otherwise provided in Section 6, a mediation communication is privileged as provided in subsection (b) and is not subject to discovery or admissible in evidence in a proceeding unless waived or precluded as provided by Section 5.

(b) In a proceeding, the following privileges apply:

    (1) A mediation party may refuse to disclose, and may prevent any other person from disclosing, a mediation communication.

    (2) A mediator may refuse to disclose a mediation communication and may prevent any other person from disclosing a mediation communication of the mediator.

    (3) A nonparty participant may refuse to disclose, and may prevent any other person from disclosing, a mediation communication of the nonparty participant.

(c) Evidence or information that is otherwise admissible or subject to discovery does not become inadmissible or protected from discovery solely by reason of its disclosure or use in a mediation.

SECTION 5. WAIVER AND PRECLUSION OF PRIVILEGE.

(a) A privilege under Section 4 may be waived in a record or orally during a proceeding if it is expressly waived by all parties to the mediation and:

 (1) in the case of the privilege of a mediator, it is expressly waived by the mediator; and

 (2) in the case of the privilege of a nonparty participant, it is expressly waived by the nonparty participant.

(b) A person that discloses or makes a representation about a mediation communication which prejudices another person in a proceeding is precluded from asserting a privilege under Section 4, but only to the extent necessary for the person prejudiced to respond to the representation or disclosure.

(c) A person that intentionally uses a mediation to plan, attempt to commit or commit a crime, or to conceal an ongoing crime or ongoing criminal activity is precluded from asserting a privilege under Section 4.

SECTION 6. EXCEPTIONS TO PRIVILEGE.

(a) There is no privilege under Section 4 for a mediation communication that is:

 (1) in an agreement evidenced by a record signed by all parties to the agreement;

(2) available to the public under open records laws or made during a session of a mediation which is open, or is required by law to be open, to the public;

(3) a threat or statement of a plan to inflict bodily injury or commit a crime of violence;

(4) intentionally used to plan a crime, attempt to commit a crime, or to conceal an ongoing crime or ongoing criminal activity;

(5) sought or offered to prove or disprove a claim or complaint of professional misconduct or malpractice filed against a mediator;

(6) except as otherwise provided in subsection (c), sought or offered to prove or disprove a claim or complaint of professional misconduct or malpractice filed against a mediation party, nonparty participant, or representative of a party based on conduct occurring during a mediation; or

(7) sought or offered to prove or disprove abuse, neglect, abandonment, or exploitation in a proceeding in which a child or adult protective services agency is a party...

Applying the tenets of the UMA, information shared during the course of a mediation, unless waived by all parties to the mediation, otherwise should be considered privileged and confidential, inadmissible for use at trial and otherwise not subject to discovery. The discussions that occur in mediation should be considered akin to the attorney-client privilege where the rights of confidentiality are strongly preserved and protected.

For those states that have not accepted the UMA, it is likely that there is a statutory alternative or at least some guidance that can be found under common law. As a practice pointer, it may be helpful for mediation agreements to reference the applicable law as to confidentiality for the jurisdiction where the mediation is to occur or at least to outline these privileges and their exceptions within the mediation agreement itself.

The Shifting Laws Relating to Non-Disclosure and Confidentiality Provisions in Settlement Agreements

Mediators who work in the employment arena helping to resolve employee claims for discrimination, harassment or retaliation are facing new challenges when it comes to the issue of including standard provisions in their settlement documents that address the confidentiality and non-disclosure of the terms of the agreement.

Typically, an employer's motivation for reaching a pre-trial settlement with its employee is to avoid the possible public disclosure of the alleged claims against the company or its employees. In fact, the ability to control the public damage of the allegations has oftentimes been a key factor in helping mediators motivate settlement.

Under new laws, found in states like California, New York and others, settlement agreements containing these confidentiality and non-disclosure provisions may be considered unenforceable. Due to public pressure to expose wrongdoers and limit their misconduct, state legislators have been amending their state laws to restrict these provisions in settlement agreements. Public opinion would suggest that such provisions may allow companies and their employers to hide their bad behavior, which otherwise would be exposed if these confidentiality and non-disclosure clauses were eliminated.

Certainly the "MeToo" movement catapulted this issue into the limelight when it was discovered that a long history of harassment may have occurred in certain companies all while being shielded from discovery through non-disclosure provisions that had been signed by employees who resolved their claims through mediation.

The difficulty with removing these provisions is that sometimes the only true incentive for an employer to settle with its claimants is exactly to help avoid the public spectacle of the disclosed claim. Employers typically will seek to avoid the negative publicity and impact to their company's goodwill that come with the public's knowledge of a company's internal disputes. Even more so, sometimes the complainant may not want the matter publicly disclosed, seeking to hide the issues from their families or the public. Some of these laws may take the right of anonymity away from the claimants themselves.

Further, federal tax Legislation has been added that prevents any tax deductions on any settlements for sexual harassment that include confidentiality provisions. Previously, a company could deduct such settlement payments as a business deduction. Under the new law if the parties include a confidentiality provision neither the employer nor the claimant can deduct their payments and costs as a deductible expense. The goal was clearly to motivate parties involved in sexual harassment claims to disclose their disputes and avoid ongoing secret settlements

Of course, mediators can help both sides in a dispute manage these pressures of the public's right to know and the personal interests of the parties involved. Mediators can work with the parties to consider alternative strategies such as permitting disclosure only by subpoena or other court action and not simply in response to media inquiry. Another approach would be to permit disclosure only if both parties are notified so as to allow each side the opportunity to present their side of the story. Lastly, mediators can work with the parties to agree to shift certain settlement amounts to other non-harassment areas (such as wage and hour claims or discrimination) which can be disclosed and therefore allowing the parties to take advantage of their expense deductions.

Ultimately, mediation is meant to allow the parties to control their circumstances and avoid the public scrutiny of litigation. Through mediation, the parties should also be able to maintain their control over the settlement process while still complying with existing law.

Depending on the state involved the parties and the mediator should explore all alternatives and options available to them to help motivate the parties to reach a resolution if that what the parties want and to do it in such a way to meet the public policy and legal requirements not to hide facts that may damage others involved. Each state's laws will undoubtedly be slightly different, even the New York law appears to allow a claimant to agree to a confidentiality provision in their settlement, at their option. Certainly, the laws should not be written in a way to punish claimants that want to avoid the potential embarrassment involved in these types of harassment disputes.

The Mediator's "Proposal": Is It Worth It?

It is certainly not that uncommon to be in a mediation where one side feels that it has moved to its "lowest number" while the other side has reached its "highest number" and the gap cannot be overcome. It is at a juncture like this where mediators can choose to insert themselves into the negotiation process by choosing to make a mediator's proposal or offer that the mediator believes will bridge the gap to help the case settle.

But by taking this action the mediator, instead of staying out of the direct negotiation of terms, places itself directly into the process. For many, it is an uncomfortable place to be as a third-party impartial participant. But is it worth it?

Some would say yes, so long as the method for making the mediator's proposal is handled carefully and skillfully. First, the proposal would only be something that would be used at the late stage of a mediation, where the parties are believed to have each reached their limits of settlement authority or willingness to move further. Second, the mediator must address their proposal in full confidentially to each party, making sure not to disclose the response by either party unless both sides are agreeable. In other words, the mediator will not disclose that one party said "yes" until both sides say "yes". That way if one party accepts and the other does not, the party that may have accepted does not lose their settlement standing when it may come to future negotiations. Third, the mediator must carefully articulate that the proposal is not meant to be an analysis of the relative merit or weakness of a particular case but merely an effort to help bridge the gap in place in the current settlement discussion. This will help avoid the misunderstanding that the mediator is expressing the worth of the case as compared to its effort to help the parties reach a settlement on a disputed matter.

Certainly, the decision to utilize a mediator's proposal must be left to the mediator's analysis of the statements and behavior observed during the specific mediation itself. Obviously, there are times when making such a proposal may be more disadvantageous than other times. But if the mediator truly believes that their effort to create such an offer might be the missing piece toward settlement, there may be no reason to hesitate.

As to the question of whether a mediator's proposal imposes an unfair influence on the parties to the mediation, the answer may depend on how the mediator's proposal is presented and further whether both sides are represented by counsel. A mediator's proposal may not be appropriate if one party is unrepresented. A mediator's proposal may also not be warranted if the respective parties are so far apart that the offer may be considered an insult to one side or demeaning to the other.

As has been often said, a good mediator carries a large toolbox of strategies and approaches to be used during a mediation to assist the adverse parties in resolving their dispute. Considering a mediator's proposal is just one more of those tools that may be appropriate to use when the situation calls for it.

Mediation as a Platform for Settlement Negotiation

Certainly, when parties are otherwise unable to reach consensus on a settlement, the decision to utilize mediation as another method to enhance discussions is oftentimes a positive choice. Mediation offers the parties a new "playing field" where each side can arrive with a new perspective on resolution. Mediation offers the opportunity to include a third party neutral to assist and facilitate those discussions and hopefully presents the parties with an equal and balanced format to allow the bargaining process to proceed without undue pressure. But the approach to the mediation by the parties is important. For a mediation to be successful, everything should be on the table and up for discussion. Flexibility should be acknowledged. The goal of resolution should be presented as a mutual objective.

It is fine to initiate a mediation with a settlement position that is realistic and supported by facts and law. It is another thing to start with a demand that is unrealistic and excessive. Typically, once a mediation starts out with an impracticable demand, it makes the other side challenged to find a response that is productive. Therefore, sometimes these opening demands only delay positive discussions. Similarly, an attitude of "hard bargaining" with negative behavior can typically lead to negative responses or can make it difficult for the other side to counter. Parties should avoid threats, demands or warnings during the process. Undeniably, that behavior typically results in reactions that are negative and non-productive. Many times, such behavior can call into the questions of the parties' rationality. If a participant appears not to be acting fairly during the process, the likelihood of resolution will be low.

As is often said, negotiation involves a bargaining "process". It is not a one-time event. The process calls for time, deliberation, and a back-and-forth approach that allows all parties involved to participate, to have a sense of control and oversight. The process also requires a sense that the parties are building trust as they are building solutions. Much of that trust appears when each side is open to creating trade-offs and compromise as compared to intractability. Generally, the best negotiations reach a mutual conclusion through small deliberate steps rather than large jumps. The back and forth in that process may be tedious but sometimes it is necessary, again as a methodology to build trust in the process. To truly be effective, offers should invite counteroffers. A party should not be put in a position to bid against itself. Offers need to be reciprocal to keep the process moving. Where mediations often fail are when the parties arrive with a "win-lose" or "take it or leave it" philosophy. If the opposite party will not respond to an offer, then they are failing to demonstrate the needed spirit of compromise, and therefore the mediation may be unsuccessful. Certainly, there may be a sense that any offer suggests weakness. But again, without a demonstration in good faith that the parties are present to reach a deal, it is inherent that offers need to be made by both sides. It should not matter who goes first or last. The attitude to create a successful mediation must be to find a "win-win" solution. If a dispute settles without further time, expense, emotional energy and impact to productivity for the parties involved, everyone will be declared a winner.

A Neutral's Role in Finalizing a Settlement

As litigants and mediators have long understood, by the time a case is resolved, the parties involved have sometimes worked for many hours on what can be a grueling process. Therefore, it is on occasion difficult at that point to start drafting a settlement agreement from scratch. It is helpful for a mediator to come to the mediation with a settlement term sheet prepared that can be used to help clarify the issues and assist the parties in creating a binding and enforceable settlement agreement.

The most challenging aspect of creating a settlement term sheet (with an expectation by the parties that they will work later on a fully drafted settlement agreement) is ensuring that the settlement reached at the mediation can be enforced, even if there is an intention to create a more complete document later. The way to accomplish this is to include clear language in the term sheet to avoid any ambiguity about the terms that are included.

Therefore, any term sheet that is to be executed by the party litigants (and their counsel) should include language that states that the parties agree to be bound by the provisions in the term sheet and that the document is "binding and enforceable". Furthermore, even though the parties have agreed to prepare a more formal settlement agreement based on the term sheet, such a formal agreement is not a condition precedent to settlement. In other words, the term sheet should clarify that, although the parties will endeavor to create a more formal agreement based on the term sheet, such a later document is not a requirement for the enforceability of the settlement. Additionally, if a later agreement is to be drafted, the term sheet should identify a deadline for the document to be prepared and executed or be waived. This avoids the possibility of extended delays in finalizing the settlement that the parties worked so hard to reach during the mediation itself.

Since the discussions during mediation are confidential, it is additionally helpful to include in the signed terms sheet that, if a dispute arises during the drafting and execution of the later settlement agreement, the parties agree that the mediator will act as the arbitrator of any such dispute and the decision made concerning any such dispute will be final.

Of course, to avoid any potential ambiguities with a settlement, it is crucial that the mediator and the litigants seek to include all material terms of the settlement as part of the term sheet. Therefore, issues as to the amount of the settlement, deadline for payment and method of payment should all be included in the term sheet. All deadline dates should flow from the date of the mediation and the signed term sheet, not from the date of execution of some later document that may or may not be finalized. Moreover, the term sheet should clarify whether there are multiple claims and causes of action, and whether all such claims are resolved or, if intended, only a partial resolution has been reached (to avoid a later claim that the full matter was settled). Furthermore, the term sheet should cover typical issues that are discussed during settlement negotiations, such as confidentiality and the remedies for breach of confidentiality. No term sheet should indicate that issues are subject to further discussion or negotiation. Instead, the term sheet should state that the terms are final and binding, even if to be incorporated into a later, more formal agreement.

Finally, it should go without saying that the term sheet itself should be signed by all parties and dated. The term sheet should include language that such signatures acknowledge the term sheet itself is binding and enforceable.

What is "Success" in a Mediation?

We've all heard it said that a successful mediation is when "everyone leaves unhappy". Certainly, the expression is intended to convey that sometimes to make a mediation work, the plaintiff gets less than they expected to receive, and the defendant pays more than they expected to pay- so everyone is unhappy. Such a sentiment may be true, but there are many metrics to establish whether a mediation has been successful.

Of course, the main intent of a mediation is to settle the parties dispute. Many would say that the final resolution of the conflict is the only goal of a mediation and if the parties settle, that's all that matters. But in certain circumstances there are inherent elements within the process of the mediation itself to measure the true success of the resolution. A few of them include the following:

1. Shared Communication.

Sometimes the only reason a dispute finally settles at mediation is that for the first time the parties are able to confront each other in a setting where they can verbally air their positions and arguments. Separate from any pleadings, discovery, depositions or motion practice that may have come before, mediations allow the parties to directly vocalize their claims against the other party, to essentially "have their day in court" without waiting for the trial. It is often the release of emotions while in mediation that finally will trigger the next step of moving towards closure. But for the opportunity to "be heard", the dispute would not otherwise have been resolved.

2. Control

One of the most significant aspects of a mediation is that there is no judge or jury to make a decision. During a mediation, the parties are given the right to control their own destinies regarding the dispute. So, for the first time since the conflict began, the litigants are finally asked what they "want to do", instead of being told that they need to answer questions in discovery or need to respond to motions. It is the first time where they may feel a direct investment in the process and therefore ultimately understand that it might be the last time where they can personally control the outcome. Having a sense of control within a process that otherwise may seem uncontrollable may be the difference between a dispute that can be stopped or continues.

3. Respect

It is absolute that one of the most important elements during a mediation is that there is a demonstration of mutual respect by the parties during the process.

Even if one side vehemently objects to the claims being brought, in that the law allows parties to bring claims, the respondent must be willing, if nothing else, to respect the process of "civil" litigation. Sometimes, just the ability of one party to present its claim without interruption or objection from the other side, may be the trigger to allow the parties to work toward resolution.

4. Cooperation

It goes without saying that it is unlikely there would have been a dispute to start with if the parties were otherwise able to cooperate to resolve the conflict. In mediation, sometimes the parties are able to create solutions that require mutual cooperation, such as agreeing to payment plans, having to sell property to obtain liquidity or even re-establishing a working relationship to complete a project. Whatever the action may be, the mutuality of recognizing that sometimes there cannot be a solution without joint cooperation (as compared to individual defiance) can be the missing element needed to solve the problem being confronted.

A mediation that includes these four elements should ultimately lead to a successful mediation. Where the parties, after recognizing that they are in an environment conducive to resolution, can leave the mediation not only knowing that they are now free from the time, expense and stress of the past dispute, but feeling as if they were active participants in the process of creating that solution.

Debate Over Opening Statements in Mediation

There is an ongoing debate over the benefits of including opening statements in mediations. Opponents claim that allowing opposing parties to make (possibly vitriolic) statements, outlining the strengths of their respective cases and the weaknesses of the opposition, is the last thing needed right before the parties attempt to resolve their dispute. Supporters contend that opening statements, when handled properly, permit each side the unique opportunity, perhaps for the first time, to personally present their stories and to hear relevant facts and law that may help to guide the parties toward the needed resolution.

The answer, as to whether to allow opening statements, can be found in the ultimate flexibility that is inherent in the alternative dispute resolution process. Before the mediation starts, a mediator has the ability to review the type of case involved, as well as the nature and demeanor of the parties and their counsel. Since not every case is the same, the mediator's analysis of that case, including the respective expectations of the parties and counsel involved, can be used to determine whether the mediation should begin with opening statements or in separate caucuses.

Certainly, many find positives in holding opening statements. One of the strongest advantages of permitting such statements might be the opportunity for the parties, who may have simply been passive observers in the proceedings thus far, to directly participate in the process and be made aware of the time and energy involved in ongoing litigation. Further, a party's participation in opening statements allows the individuals involved to have their voices heard, which may itself be a significant component in the settlement process. Many times, certain parties are only seeking "to be heard" or to "have their day in court". Having the party participate in opening statements helps to meet this need and can oftentimes create further opportunities for settlement.

If handled correctly, a joint session with opening statements may restore the intended civility that should be part of such litigation. If the statements are cordial and the parties are able to meet face to face, it may help to diffuse any hostility that existed as a cause of the original dispute, as well as to ease any acrimony that may have developed during the preceding litigation.

Opening statements may allow for the parties to share their positions in a confidential environment and convey the evidence that may help to better instruct the parties on their respective risks of litigation. Obviously, opening statements can help to directly educate the mediator.

Listening to opening statements and the recitation of the main factual and legal issues in the dispute might provide needed insight for the mediator who is charged with helping the parties reach a resolution. Finally, joint session opening statements may assist in the consideration of some of the intangibles of the case, including the quality of the lawyers involved and the effectiveness of the parties as potential witnesses at trial.

Of course, there is the other side of the coin. If handled aggressively, opening statements could easily derail a potentially successful mediation. Tone is crucial in the delivery of the opening statements. If the opening statements are argumentative, rather than conciliatory, they may create further animosity and distance between the parties, taking what would otherwise be an opportunity for discourse and dialogue and replacing it with a situation where scorched earth becomes the goal.

At the end of the day, if the parties and the mediator agree to participate in joint opening statements, here are a few guidelines to consider:

1. Brevity is important. Franklin Delano Roosevelt once said, "Be sincere; be brief; be seated". The same is true for opening statements.
2. Use the time to thank the other side for participating and demonstrate appreciation for their decision to participate in mediation. It is true that most cases will settle, especially those

that participate in this type of alternative dispute resolution approach.

3. Visuals add to a presentation and power point programs are often successful. "A picture is worth a thousand words."

4. You can be an advocate for your client but try to avoid finger-pointing or negative assertions in your opening statements. At this point in the case, the facts are the facts. Arguing them as a method to inflame or insult the other party will fail to motivate the parties toward a successful resolution.

The Importance of Communication in Mediations

One of the main reasons that mediations fail is the lack of open communication between the parties. It is essential for both parties who voluntarily enter into the effort at resolution through mediation to have the opportunity to be heard on their concerns and needs which led them to litigation. It is equally important for the disputing parties to hear the other side of those interests. It is through that open dialogue that the parties can, possibly for the first time, recognize the issues that divide them which may create the opportunity for the parties to focus on ways to solve those issues.

Mediation is crafted to allow for open communication. That is why mediations are confidential, so as to allow the parties and their counsel an opportunity to honestly present the facts and claims to the other side so that both parties can consider each sides strengths and weaknesses. Mediation also is often the first time since the dispute arose for the parties to meet, which often presents the opportunity for direct discussion towards resolution without fear of either side using statements that are made against the other.

The communication, whether through the mediator, through counsel or through the parties directly must be in done in good faith, and must be non-judgmental to be successful. It is in those situations where one side or the other is unwilling to listen to the other where mediation cannot be successful. Communication is also not always verbal. The parties must be willing to convey their non-verbal messages in a respectful and non-judgmental way as well.

Communication is also essential when it comes to conveying proposals for settlement. Certainly there are elements of negotiation which cannot be ignored as part of the settlement process. But for a mediation to truly be successful the communication that is made, both in settlement offers and in advocacy of their positions, must be presented seriously with a goal of crafting solutions to resolve the dispute. As many mediators and lawyers know, money is not always the only element of a mediated solution. As such, both sides must listen carefully and be prepared to consider creative remedies to reach positive solutions.

Finally, it is essential that the mediator that is selected provide the trust needed to create the environment for this communication. In that much of the communication happens between the mediator and the parties separately, it is crucial that the parties feel that their messages and offers are properly being communicated by the mediator to the other side. As is sometimes the case, the success of a mediation depends not only on the words that are spoken, but oftentimes on the way they are presented by the mediator. And as is always the case, listening is a crucial part of the communication process as well.

Why Do Mediations Fail?

There are dozens of reasons why disputes that should be able to be resolved at a mediation sometimes fail. One reason may be that the mediator selected was not the right person for the type of dispute involved. Another may be that the attorneys involved were not fully prepared and that lack of preparation impacted the willingness of the parties to move from their original positions. Another might be that the parties themselves simply did not attend the mediation in good faith, ready, willing and able to settle the dispute.

The empirical evidence about mediations is that they generally are very successful in resolving disputes. The number of successful settlements in mediation often times rank in the 80-90 percent range. But again, sometimes cases do not settle.

Those that have been involved in mediations over the years generally know the difference between good and bad mediators. Mediators that simply shuttle offers between the parties tend to have far less success than those that foster communication between the parties. Similarly, those mediators that fail to help clarify the issues in dispute, fail to explore the true interests of the parties or fail to help to craft meaningful solutions to problems will commonly have less success than those that fail to participate in the process of resolution and the hard work that goes with it. Good mediators should facilitate communication between the parties, analyze the people and situations that led to the dispute and work with the parties to find solutions.

Attorneys that fail to prepare for mediations can often be responsible for their failure as well. Most importantly lawyers must prepare their clients for what will happen in a mediation, the time it will take, the importance of participating in the process as well as acknowledging that to be successful the parties must be willing to move from their respective positions. The attorneys must engage all involved parties in the mediation, including insurance companies that are potentially liable, whether subrogation or contribution will be an element of the resolution and should verify the financial settlement authority of the parties that the lawyer is representing. All of this is separate from preparing the presentation of the facts and law needed to sway the other parties involved so that they consider the risk of litigation. The lawyers should have all of their evidence available at the mediation and a clear understanding of their eventual trial strategy. Without a demonstration of a strong case by the parties involved, mediation won't be successful simply because neither side will feel as if they have risk in going to court.

Lastly, the parties themselves must be participants in good faith. Especially when the mediation is voluntary and not court ordered, the participants must be emotionally present to attend the mediation with a goal of resolution. If the parties attending enter the mediation overconfident, and appear at the mediation only for "free discovery", the process will likely not work. A recalcitrant party, unwilling to be flexible and unwilling to move from their stated position or change their financial offer, will undoubtedly lead to an impasse. For mediation to truly work the parties themselves, the central figures in deciding to settle or fight further, must be in the mindset to be open-minded for resolution. Otherwise, the effort at mediation will be wasted.

The Psychology of Mediations

If we were to look at why conflicts develop between individuals or even companies, it is likely due simply because of differing opinions between the parties. Those differing opinions can be due to the disputing party's frame of reference to a situation as compared to their intentional effort to challenge the other party. Everyone has their own values, needs, experiences and cultures, which creates the frame of reference by which we view things. It is these differences which must be explored in order to reach a resolution in many disputes. Mediation – or the non-adversarial style of dispute resolution- is oftentimes the best way to allow the parties to explore those differences and permit the parties to reach a meaningful resolution of their conflict.

Recognizing that parties enter into conflicts this way – essentially because they feel that they are "right" and the other person is "wrong" – is a key to approaching how the dispute can be resolved. Once a mediator understands that the conflict is based on the differences of the parties' frame of reference, the mediator can seek to intervene to help both sides find a mutual solution to the dispute. In other words, a good mediator can use the parties differing frames of reference to find an answer to the problem.

Disputes can also be very emotional for the parties involved and all parties handle their emotions differently. Therefore, how the parties communicate is commonly a significant element in the potential success of the mediation. The emotion of the parties must be tested by the mediator involved in the matter. Some parties avoid confrontation while others seek it. Some parties respond better to a sympathetic tone rather than to an aggressive one. A good mediator should be able to hopefully gauge whether the parties should talk together or separately and even whether the lawyers should talk directly or only through the mediator.

At the end of the day, even if the dispute involves money, as long as people are making the decisions they will be impacted by their own set of values and opinions as well as their own unique set of emotions. All of this must be considered by a good mediator to help the parties find accord to reach a resolution of their dispute. Sometimes simply the recognition that the parties themselves can ultimately control the outcome of their dispute may be the strongest motivator for parties to seek resolution by mediation rather than to risk a decision by an arbitrator, judge or jury.

Why Mediations and Arbitrations Are More Important Now Than Ever Before

As litigators of all types, in all areas of the law, in big or small firms, we all collectively suffer with the closure of our public courthouses during this virus crisis. Cases are stayed, parties are frustrated and there seems to be a lack of control to create solutions to the growing needs of our clients. Further, it seems clear that even when this crisis has passed, whenever that may be, the backlog of cases will be overwhelming. Clerks and judges will struggle to accommodate their dockets to manage not only the cases that have been pending, but the new litigation that will erupt as a result of this emergency. As litigators representing our clients, we consistently seek a fair and efficient resolution of our matters. Now we are experiencing an obstacle in our way to accomplishing this goal for our clients.

Now, more than ever, especially as public dispute resolution is impacted, the shift to private alternative dispute resolution (ADR) seems to be a clear alternative to helping parties in litigation reach closure of their pending matters.

<u>Mediation</u>. Think about the independent stressors that now exist for the parties on both sides of any pending dispute. Each may be struggling with multiple concerns such as business survival, the financial welfare of their family, or bank lending that may be hindered by having pending litigation, and a host of other factors that may not have been present when the case was initially filed. We all know the pressure that exists between parties regardless of whether the matter is a personal injury dispute or a business contract dispute. Whereas the parties may have staunchly objected in the past to "sitting in the room" with the other party to work out their differences, times have now changed. Private mediation, outside of the court system, must be a consideration for all parties in litigation. Again, although it is a non-binding process, it has a higher than 80% success rate. This is a time, whatever service or mediator you choose, to take advantage of the reality that the mediation process is a vital option for your clients.

<u>Arbitration</u>. So, your client wants its day in court with a decision-maker. But how long are they willing to wait to get that to happen? Arbitration is simply a private alternative to court. Arbitration laws have been created to provide for a final binding award without extensive docket delays. The parties can opt for discovery and motion practice if they so choose. If the matter is unique as to an area of law, an arbitrator can be selected from that particular field. If the parties believe that one

arbitrator is insufficient for a fair hearing and resolution, a panel can be selected. There is a wide variety of options within the arbitration process that should allow parties to mutually agree on this alternative, even if the parties' contract does not call for arbitration. Keep in mind that even if a case is in mid-progress, the parties can still mutually agree to stay their case pending arbitration. And an arbitrator can be directed to acknowledge and proceed in the pending case bound by any initial rulings from the Court as a starting point for their proceedings.

Virtual ADR. Lastly, mediation and arbitration services are making themselves available during our shelter-in-place compliance with easily available technology to allow these proceedings to continue. Many of us have been using video conferencing for the first time ever and recognize that it does provide a personal (albeit "virtual") connection to others. The same applies to the use of this technology in mediations and arbitrations. But the use of live video technology is just one option that can be used. Keep in mind that mediations have regularly included telephonic connections and have been successful in doing so. Similarly, arbitrations have for years offered "document submission" resolutions or hearings through telephone. Not every case prior to this crisis was mediated or arbitrated only in live hearings.

As we have all learned recently, we need to adapt to succeed. Working from home is just the start. Cases still need to be tried; clients need to be helped. ADR is a true solution.

Is Mediation the Same Thing as Meditation?

The terms are often confused, but they are not the same. Mediation is, of course, a method of alternative dispute resolution where the litigating parties select a third party neutral to guide them through a negotiation process towards the settlement of their dispute. Meditation is often defined as a practice of mindfulness, used to reduce stress, find focus and peace or to reach a heightened level of spiritual connection.

Are they different? Yes. But surprisingly meditation can be a component of a successful mediation practice and methodology. There is no doubt that in order to engage in a meaningful process of dispute resolution through mediation, the parties must be willing to be "present" during the discussion process. It is very difficult to have a successful mediation where the parties involved are angry and combative. Finding a place where the parties are fully engaged and focused on the task at hand is an essential element in reaching a successful result. Mindfulness, or seeking a place of calm, peace, balance or relaxation, is a perfect state of mind from which to participate in a mediation, the ultimate goal of which is to reach a peaceful solution and compromise of positions.

Mediation offers an opportunity for parties locked in a dispute to discuss and consider creative solutions towards resolution. In a court proceeding there are only "winners" and "losers", whereas in mediation the parties retain control and have the ability to be innovative in their solution strategies. Finding mindfulness during the mediation process can have profound positive effects. Mindfulness assists with greater cognitive ability, managing fatigue and improving decision making. A meditative approach during mediation can assist with reducing stress and increasing the participant's focus and concentration so that the parties may truly contribute their full attention to the settlement process.

Meditation can be a helpful tool to assist the parties in reaching a proper frame of mind for open discussion and reasonable consideration of the issues that led them to the current dispute, as well as a place of self-determination to settle their conflict. Meditation may not help the participants reach a perfect place of "Zen" during a mediation. But if the parties can find a place of comfort wherein to end their dispute, the resulting avoidance of ongoing stress, risk, cost and expense may in fact be the best place for the parties involved. That type of closure may itself be considered a "successful" mediation.

Not only is a meditative state helpful for the parties during a mediation, but a mediator who can also find a place of balance in its evaluative considerations can better help the parties towards their goal of resolution. A mediator who can reduce their own stress and increase their own focus during a mediation will be better able to help the parties involved reach a state of acceptance and peace. A good mediator is typically a person who is able to "read the room", has acute awareness of the basis of the conflict, can create calm in unnerving situations, offers laughter as a method of stress relief, and can evoke sensitivity and sympathy in the context of the setting. These are often similar skills to those of one who understands the role of meditation and how it can reduce stress, expand insight and improve clarity. Bringing meditation into the mediation process can ultimately enhance the mediator's opportunity to help find a connection or bridge of commonality between the disputing parties.

The Dynamics of "Power" in a Mediation

The issue of relative power as part of the mediation process can get very complicated. Each party comes to a mediation with certain advantages and disadvantages, whether related to the procedural status of the lawsuit (pending motions to dismiss or evidentiary rulings that may weigh in favor of one party versus the other), the merits of the case (lack of witnesses, lack of documentation), the financial ability of each party to cover the cost of extended litigation or even the psychological ability of each party to manage the stress of litigation.

Interestingly, there are even further issues of power that can apply to a mediation, including social media pressures on the parties relating to the dispute, cultural issues associated with being involved in a dispute or even the personal traits of the individual parties (including each party's race, sex, national origin or sexual orientation). All of these issues may carry weight in the balancing of power, especially when the parties also factor in the designated trier of fact, whether it be a judge, a jury or an arbitrator. Each of these power issues must be considered in the management of the mediation and may ultimately impact the eventual ability for the matter to be resolved.

Why is the element of power important? Because power is generally defined as the ability to influence the behavior of others. In mediation it is important to "level the playing field" for the parties involved to avoid an imbalance of power of one party over another party.

And then there is the subtle issue of the power of the mediator. Is the mediator acting simply as a messenger, shuttling offers for consideration between the disputing parties or is the mediator a subject matter expert in the field, offering an evaluative analysis of the pending dispute? Depending on the role of the mediator, the neutral must be able to carefully wield its power, not to influence either party to reach a settlement, but to control the attempted exercise of power between the two disputing parties. If a mediator is able to manage any imbalance of power during a negotiation, the mediator's ability to bring the conflict towards a resolution will be enhanced.

Again, power can come into play from numerous sources: the power of resources, the power of status and the power of emotion. The relative strength of those powers often becomes significant based on the context of the dispute, but often the power asserted by one party may be detrimental to the ability to find closure for the conflict. A mediator should be able to shift the dynamics of power in a dispute so that there is a balance between the parties. This balance will help the parties find a point of resolution for the dispute. While a true balance of power in a mediation may be impossible, the effort to seek such a balance must be made. Absent such a balance, the asserted power of one party over the other may simply result in the failure of a resolution.

How can a mediator create such a balance? The mediator should endeavor to give each party the equal right to speak or otherwise engage in the mediation or negotiating process; the mediator should allow each party to share, in confidence, the strengths and weaknesses of their case without fear of disclosure; and the mediator should avoid any circumstances where any party feels pressured or coerced to present or accept any offer to resolve the case.

The dynamics of power in mediation can be challenging. Every party comes to the mediation table with different strengths and weaknesses and, although a true balance of power may be hard to achieve, if the effort is made to create an environment of fairness, the chance of reaching a resolution of the pending conflict becomes greater.

Enforcing Arbitration Provision in Contracts: What's the Law Today?

It is hard to keep track of the differing opinions coming out of the Federal Court of Appeals and the Supreme Court on the issue of the enforcement of arbitration provisions in different types of contracts as well as the ability to include a class action waiver as part of that arbitration dispute remedy.

In 2011, the United States Supreme Court ruled in AT&T Mobility v. Concepcion that the Federal Arbitration Act (FAA) makes arbitration agreements valid, including those with class action waivers. The court ruled similarly in the case of CompuCredit Corp. v. Greenwood in 2012 and in American Express Co., v. Italian Colors Restaurant in 2013. Both those cases appeared to strengthen the policy supporting arbitration provisions in contracts. It would have seemed then that the issue regarding the enforceability of those arbitration agreements with class action waivers had been resolved.

But in 2012, the National Labor Relations Board rendered an opinion in the case of D. R. Horton that arbitration provisions with class action waivers violated section 7 of the National Labor Relation Act (NLRA) which protects a worker's ability to "engage in other concerted activities". That language, the NLRB claims, would arguably include the ability of employees to participate in class action litigation as compared to having to file individual arbitration claims to resolve their disputes.

Until recently, the D.R. Horton rule had been rejected by every appellate court to consider it. For example, the Fifth Circuit Court of Appeals (covering Texas, Louisiana, Mississippi) in the case of NLRB v. Murphy Oil, USA (2015) held that the NLRB was wrong to determine that arbitration provisions with class actions waivers violated the NLRA. Similarly, the Second Circuit Court of Appeals (covering New York, Connecticut and Vermont) in the case of Sutherland v. Ernst & Young (2013) and the Eighth Circuit (covering Arkansas) in the case of Cellular Sales of Missouri v. NLRB (2016) rejected the NLRB's reasoning and chose to enforce the class action waivers in the arbitration agreements presented to the Court.

But the Seventh Circuit Court of Appeals (covering Illinois, Indiana, Wisconsin) in the case of Epic Systems v. Lewis (2016) and the Ninth Circuit Court of Appeals (California, Arizona, Alaska) in the case of Ernst & Young v. Morris (2016) reached decisions *agreeing* with the NRLB and concluded that the requirement to arbitrate disputes between employers and employees was unenforceable.

The Supreme Court granted certiorari in three of the cases, <u>Murphy Oil, Epic Systems and Ernst and Young</u>, since there was a split of opinion among the circuit courts on this one issue. Oral arguments were held on October 2, 2017.

Certainly, it is clear why arbitration agreements are desired by employers. There has been a significant growth in class action litigation over the last few years, both in the employment and consumer contexts. Arbitration agreements, with class action waivers, provide a strategy to avoid the expense and risk of class action disputes. Employers see arbitration as a quicker and more efficient method of resolving disputes since matters can be handled on an individual basis compared to class actions which may include hundreds if not thousands of alleged parties. Also, arbitrations can be handled privately compared to court and often with faster results, which employers argue benefits both sides. Further, there is less risk of appeal and more control by the individual plaintiffs, who might otherwise, in class action litigation, be limited in their rights of settlement. All of this is in addition to the arguments that class actions are known for abuse such as parties receiving little recovery while counsel for the cases receive substantial fees. There is also the concern that class actions may obscure the rights of individual parties who may have stronger cases then the plaintiff class as a whole.

But there appears more at stake than just whether arbitration is a better option than court litigation. The bigger question, especially in the cases being heard by the Supreme Court, is whether the NLRA can supersede the enforceability of the Federal Arbitration Act. The NLRB, in following the NLRA, contends that the action of enforcing an arbitration provision with a class action waiver against an employee seeking redress against its employer is patently an "unfair labor practice". As it stands now, parties with an arbitration agreement would be compelled to arbitrate their dispute unless the FAA's rules have been "overridden by contrary congressional command" (one of the exceptions in the FAA). In the cases now being argued before the Supreme Court, the defense has been that there is no demonstration of any congressional command that would outweigh the enforceability of these companies' arbitration agreements. It's also interesting to note that even where the court might suggest that these arbitration agreements with class action waivers might be violative of public policy or fairness, the court has still found that those arguments do not overcome the "direct, controlling authority" that such agreements, including class action waivers, must be enforced under the law. Essentially, since the creation of the Federal Arbitration Act in 1925, arbitrations have been recognized as an efficient, cost effective and faster method of dispute resolution compared to the judicial jury system.

As this dispute continues, and all parties anxiously await the Supreme Court's ruling on these three cases, there are certain things that can be done to minimize the argument that the employer is acting with an unfair advantage when it comes to employee dispute resolution. First, the provisions dealing with dispute resolution should be highlighted or even drafted as a standalone document to avoid an argument that the arbitration provision was not clear and obvious. Second, the arbitration agreement should be mutual, so that both parties are similarly obligated to handle their disputes through arbitration. Third, employers or businesses should agree to pay for the cost of the arbitration. Since arbitration is private and not public there is a cost to the process which is not required in court matters. As such, without financial support, the likelihood of a claim being filed by an individual litigant may be impracticable. Arbitration provisions may be seen to be more favorable if the employer or business involved agrees to pay the fees and costs for the benefit of both parties.

Other recommendations include allowing the employee or consumer to opt of the arbitration agreement when the contract is signed or including specific clarity as to what type of claims would fall under the arbitration provision or may be classified as matters that would be better suited for court resolution. One such example is to permit court actions where the dispute involved falls under the jurisdictional level of the smalls claims courts for the state where the dispute occurs.

The pundits assume, especially with the current make-up of the Supreme Court, that the previous decisions favoring the FAA will prevail. But even with that hopeful mindset, it makes sense for employers and businesses selling to the public to review their current arbitration provisions to ensure that they are presented clearly and fairly.

Vacating an Arbitration Award under the Federal Arbitration Act or the Georgia Arbitration Act.

Under 9 U.S.C.A. §10 of the Federal Arbitration Act, an award may be vacated under four specific grounds:

(1) where the award was procured by corruption, fraud, or undue means;

(2) where there was evident partiality or corruption in the arbitrators, or either of them;

(3) where the arbitrators were guilty of misconduct in refusing to postpone the hearing, upon sufficient cause shown, or in refusing to hear evidence pertinent and material to the controversy; or of any other misbehavior by which the rights of any party have been prejudiced; or

(4) where the arbitrators exceeded their powers, or so imperfectly executed them that a mutual, final, and definite award upon the subject matter submitted was not made.

Under O.C.G.A. §9-9-13 of the Georgia Arbitration Act, an award may be vacated under five specific grounds:

(1) Corruption, fraud, or misconduct in procuring the award;

(2) Partiality of an arbitrator appointed as a neutral;

(3) An overstepping by the arbitrators of their authority or such imperfect execution of it that a final and definite award upon the subject matter submitted was not made;

(4) A failure to follow the procedure of this part, unless the party applying to vacate the award continued with the arbitration with notice of this failure and without objection; or

(5) The arbitrator's manifest disregard of the law.

As can be readily seen, the Georgia Arbitration Act recognizes that "manifest disregard" of the law is an independent ground for overturning an arbitration award compared to the Federal Act which does not include the "manifest disregard" as a ground for vacatur.

Based on past decisions, O.C.G.A. §9-9-13(5) has been interpreted narrowly, requiring "clear evidence that the arbitrator intended to purposefully disregard the law." America's Home Place, Inc. v. Cassidy, 301 Ga. App. 233, 687 Ga. App. 254 (Ga. App. 2009).

There have even been cases that required a "transcript or findings of fact in the arbitrator's award" to be sufficient evidence to support a finding of manifest disregard. First Option Mortgage, LLC v. S&S Financial Mortgage Corp. 322 Ga. App. 14, 743 S.E. 2d 574 (Ga. App. 2013).

Most recently, in Adventure Motorsports Reinsurance, Ltd. v. Interstate National Dealer Services, Inc. 356 Ga. App. 236, 846 S.E. 2d 115 (Ga. App. 2020), the Court held that the "arbitrator manifestly disregarded the law by explicitly rejecting the contractual language." The Court found then that the Superior Court had erred by confirming the arbitration award and reversed the Superior Court's Judgment.

This is compared to findings that applied the Federal Arbitration Act. The Supreme Court has held "It is only when an arbitrator strays from interpretation and application of the agreement and effectively dispenses his own brand of industrial justice that his decision may be unenforceable." Stolt-Nielson S.A. v. AnimalFeeds Int'l Corp. 130 S. Ct 1758 (2010), see also Hall Street Associates, LLC v. Mattel, Inc. 128 S. Ct. 1396 (2008).

However, notwithstanding the Supreme Court holdings, the Circuit Courts have split on their grounds for vacating arbitration awards. Currently, based on past decisions, the Fifth, Eighth and Eleventh Circuits continue to hold that manifest disregard of the law is not an applicable basis for vacating an arbitration award as compared to the Second, Fourth, Seventh, Ninth and Tenth Circuits which have taken the opposite view and have elected to consider manifest disregard as a basis to overturn an arbitrator's award. The First, Sixth and Third Circuits have remained undecided on the issue notwithstanding decisions that have recognized the grounds for manifest disregard for the law as a basis for vacatur as a "high standard".

How a court may enforce an award in arbitration may factor into the election of whether to pursue arbitration under the Federal Arbitration Act or your State's Arbitration Act and whether to seek confirmation of the award under the Federal Arbitration Act or the applicable state law. As can be seen, both state law and federal law are constantly evolving as to the appropriate standard for enforcing an award.

Negotiating Between a
Rock and a Hard Place

There are times when two parties come to a mediation without any interest in settlement. Typically, this is the result of a court ordered mediation where the parties are forced to meet to discuss their case as opposed to those matters where the parties voluntarily elect to mediate based on an expectation and interest in reaching a resolution.

In the former situation, a mediator may find themselves literally between a "rock", a party unwilling and uninterested in any movement and a "hard place", a party who is unwavering in its fortitude and unrelenting in its position. So, what is a mediator to do in such a situation?

If the parties are brought together to discuss "settlement" or "compromise" in a strongly contested dispute, sometimes it is impossible for either side to change its position out of concern that any willingness to compromise their respective position might suggest to the other side an acknowledgement of a possible weakness in their case.

To avoid this potential impasse, it is strongly suggested that a mediator focus the parties on simply participating in the "process" of mediation. It can sometimes be easier for parties to find a connection to mediation if they understand it as being one part of the litigation process, not simply a methodology for the parties to negotiate a settlement.

And such a description of mediation would be an honest one because mediation is now considered a common part of the litigation process. Simply put, mediation is an effort to allow the parties to discuss the relative merits of their case at a juncture in the litigation where they can honestly access the strengths and weaknesses of their case and use the mediation process as an opportunity to take control of where the case is heading. Even though a mediation may not end up where the mediator hoped, not all cases can be settled. But, if the parties are given the opportunity of self-determination, a case that is stagnant and idle in terms of resolution can be re-ignited through discussions with the appointed neutral. Remember, those conversations don't need to be about compromise. They can be conversations about reality testing, expectations of costs and fees, the lengthy durations of trial dockets, stress from ongoing discovery and depositions, the evaluation of related law or a myriad of other areas rather than simply forced movement in settlement positions. Participating in the "practice" of mediation may be enough to initiate some migration of the parties' respective offers.

These days mediation can be viewed merely as an opportunity to discuss offers and counteroffers through an independent messenger. But in truth, mediation can also be explained and implemented as an important piece in the progression of a lawsuit. And if the parties understand that participation in mediation is part of a process, either voluntary or court ordered, there may be a greater chance that any negotiations within that proceeding will be successful.

In other words, there is a way to move outside of the rock and the hard place, but it may require the mediator to remove the constraints of the parties' positions, taking them outside the confines of their claims and counterclaims and more into the process or practice of mediation itself.

The Goal of "Closure" in Mediation

Disputes are stressful. It doesn't matter whether the conflict is personal or business, disputes cost time and money. But they also incur a psychological cost to the parties. These external pressures, even more than the merits of the dispute itself, often drive the parties to seek a resolution of their case. Mediation is the perfect process, acting as constant motivation, driving the parties toward conciliation and resolution, and, as a result, removing some of those external stressors.

For a mediator, recognizing the extent of these external stress factors can help ease the quarreling parties closer to settlement. A discussion of the benefits of "closure", a true conclusion of any ongoing dispute over the issues, can sometimes be the central theme, allowing the parties to fully engage in the mediation process.

But the discussion of the benefits of closure may be best left to the confidentiality of private break-out sessions. Often an acknowledgment or admission of stress by one party may be used by the other side of the dispute to exploit the suffering party. So, notwithstanding the mutual benefits of a resolution, a mediator needs to use caution in determining how and when to address the personal impacts of the dispute so as not to sway the outcome of the dispute toward one party or the other.

Regardless of whether a dispute is personal or business-related, the concept of closure inherently brings with it the perspective of "hope" or "aspiration", the idea that the cessation of the pending dispute will create an opportunity for a fresh start, a clean break and movement toward a more positive place. Often times, pending litigation can result in stagnation until the dispute is resolved. For a business, this may mean a delay in investment for the company, an inability to close a loan or ongoing uncertainty regarding future hiring. When the matter is personal, the unresolved dispute could affect the ability of a party to relocate, find a new job or pursue an ongoing relationship. Only with closure of the pending dispute can the affected parties begin to focus their attention on the pursuit of the next steps beyond the current matter.

These motivational concepts, psychological in nature, inevitably play a part in why parties are willing to consider alternative dispute resolution and why ADR methods, like mediation, can be so successful. The need for closure is a personal trait that many of us share. Mediation is simply a process that can be employed to work toward resolution, thereby helping the parties in a dispute reach that desirable goal.

"We Were on a Break!": Strategically Calling for an Intermission During a Mediation

One of the most famous storylines from the sitcom "Friends" is where Ross and Rachel suffer through a break-up in their relationship only to end up together at the end of the series (hopefully, no spoilers there). Interestingly, in a number of recent mediations, rather than push through extended late hours in ongoing conversations and forcing a final draft of an exhausting (and somewhat exasperating) settlement memorandum, the parties agreed to "take a break" and return again another day to conclude the mediation. Sometimes the return was the next day and sometimes the return was a week or more later. The returns have been both in person and virtual, but in every instance, the parties dutifully returned to complete the settlement process. In other words, taking the break did not interrupt or interfere with the closure of the settlement but instead, may have been the reason the cases were able to settle.

Simply put, mediations can be exhausting, not just for the parties and their lawyers, but oftentimes for the mediator as well. Depending on the complexity of the dispute and the relative positions of the parties, mediations can be both physically and emotionally debilitating. There are often times in mediations when the parties can no longer push themselves to reach a settlement, no matter how close they may be. In lieu of issuing an impasse, a mediator should feel comfortable suggesting that the parties simply "take a break", if not just for the night, maybe for a few days or sometimes even longer, especially if significant facts related to the case may influence the settlement (pending court orders, project repairs, parties otherwise unavailable). Whatever the situation may be, it can be very productive for the parties to call an intermission in their session and reconvene later, again either in person or virtually, to pick up where they left off and work towards a negotiated closure of the dispute.

There is, of course, a school of thought which recommends that, once the decision makers are all in the same room, they should be pushed to finish the mediation in one continuous meeting, whether they settle or not. And, in many circumstances that is the correct approach. But sometimes, depending on the situation, the better option would be to let the parties enjoy a recess from the pressure of the moment and reconvene later. If nothing else, the option for an intermission should be one of the tools in a mediator's toolbelt. Offering a recess should not be seen as a failure of the process but rather as an element of the practice of dispute resolution. Such a decision could be made depending on the condition of the parties, their lawyers and the mediator and the status of the negotiations themselves. If a resolution is close, it is certainly best to finish. But sometimes, like with Ross and Rachel, the parties can still succeed even after a "break up".

Will Artificial Intelligence Technology Ever Really Replace Mediation?

Artificial Intelligence in the world of law is rapidly impacting how research and writing can be accomplished. AI is also accelerating the gathering of data and how it is applied. The question is, could all of that information be used to help disputing parties settle their claims without the need for a third party neutral?

It is an interesting question, especially since the tipping point for case resolution can often be based on the financial range of jury verdict decisions in similar cases. If data were gathered on similar cases and AI could calculate the range of what a particular case might be "worth," would both sides simply be willing to settle within that offered range? Would confidential discussions and shuttle negotiation by a third-party neutral still be needed?

Many in the mediation world accept the fact that AI-guided mediation may be possible in simple "rear-end" vehicle accidents where the cost of vehicle repair can be readily determined and the range of limited medical services fees can be considered. At the same time, those same mediators believe that in other cases, where the facts are not consistent and the law subjective, AI may be helpful, but cannot replace the role of a skilled mediator who must collaborate with the adverse parties to ultimately reach a resolution. One needs to remember that a mediator must often cope with significant emotional and psychological issues that impact party litigants. AI is not currently capable of dealing with such matters. Although AI may provide important data in the course of a mediation, it cannot convey the empathy often needed to create honest and open communication between the parties. AI certainly cannot "problem-solve" the way humans can in offering creative, relevant solutions to bridge unique gaps in dispute resolution.

Undoubtedly the legal industry will ultimately benefit from the services that AI can provide, especially as it relates to the processing of data. But knowing the numbers does not substitute for the intangible skills of a human when working with disputing adversaries in attempting to reach consensus. AI may be good, but it is not yet ready to replace the unique characteristics of human interaction, especially when the parties involved have diverse and conflicting positions.

But time will tell.

About the Author

Certified Mediator and Arbitrator Scott Zucker specializes in business and commercial litigation with an emphasis on dispute resolution in the areas of construction, real estate, employment, landlord-tenant and franchise law. Scott represents companies in matters relating to contract claims, loss and damage claims, delay and productivity claims, premises liability actions and tenant dispossessory.

For over thirty-five years, Scott Zucker has acted as outside legal counsel to a variety of privately held and publicly traded businesses involved in multiple industries. As a primary litigator, Scott understands the pros and cons of pursuing, as well as defending, claims between individuals and companies.

His legal services have ranged from handling general corporate matters and providing risk management advice to companies as well as the representation of clients in the litigation or arbitration of contract disputes, insurance coverage claims, construction defects, premises liability, employment termination actions and environmental matters. Scott's goal is to apply his experience and knowledge to help contending parties reach resolutions of their disputes as efficiently and economically as possible.

Scott is a founding partner of the law firm Weissmann Zucker Euster + Katz P.C. and is actively involved in the ADR community, having served as Chairman of the Dispute Resolution Section of the Atlanta Bar Association and Chairman of the Dispute Resolution Section for the State Bar of Georgia. His mediation service, Epic Resolution Services, was founded in 2015.

Scott obtained his undergraduate degree from Washington University in St. Louis, in 1984, and his law degree from George Washington University in Washington, D.C, in 1987.

Printed in the United States
by Baker & Taylor Publisher Services